All of my Snipple Snapples

All of my Snipple Snapples

Leon McConnell

Resist Entertainment
2019

Copyright © 2019 by Resist Entertainment

All rights reserved. This book or any portion thereof may not be reproduced or used in any manner whatsoever without the express written permission of the publisher except for the use of brief quotations in a book review or scholarly journal.

First Printing: 2019
ISBN 978-0-578-56958-1
Resist Entertainment
Boyle Heights, California

Cover Art & Logo by Sergio D. Robleto
Graphic Design by Prince Johnson

Part 1:

When you look at a person all you see is the packaging. It's nutty how many people are in love with the packaging.

One day a pretty smile will catch your eye and their jokes will make you laugh and love will have its havoc and everything between these hearts will look like chaos.

You can't imagine all the things you don't know. Yet somehow, you're so certain that everything you think you know is true.

Let's not worry about having to agree. You be you and I'll be me.

So much of everything is trying to be something. But I'm not trying to be anything at all.

Bed is a language that doesn't translate well outside its borders.

You're undervaluing your assets because you're driven by your impulses.

It's not that I'm drowning. It's that I've learned to live underwater.

A good tongue can find its way from a softly bitten thigh to a nice warm home in one long lick.

Let's drive to the ocean and run into the water, throwing our clothes off as we go.

Gold dust sunshine from slat vents flecks crevices and floats deep into skin walls.

Love is accepting someone as they are but wanting them to be their best.

What if moths are just the ghosts of butterflies trying to find their way into the light?

All of my Snipple Snapples

What's sad is that your life is built on lies. What's worse is that the biggest liar is you.

Having been all around the world, I've learned that the most exotic place you could be is often somewhere in the person right next to you.

There are no safe adventures.

My kind of people are the ones who don't have much interest in being anyone's kind of anything.

If love is a thorn in your finger then life is but a trickle of blood.

So many of the problems amongst humans and between humans and nature stem from creating distinctions between man and nature, between humans and humanity, between god and existence. If one held the view that god is in all, then man, existence and all of humanity would flow harmoniously.

The philosopher in me says communication is relative to the intent of the speaker but the elementary school graduate in me wishes you would learn how to form sentences using proper grammar, punctuation and spelling.

People idealize the past because it's full of times you could never go back to, people you could never meet now, and a person you could never be again. We all want what we can't have.

May your day be kind and lovely ...and may you be the same.

Over time I've become so jaded. It's heart breaking. I'm on the decline. Man, I can feel my spark fading.

Art is the fruit of life not the point of it but life is so much sweeter when you take time to enjoy some nice fruit.

There's one person for everyone out there, who can complete you, give your life meaning and make you whole. It's yourself.

If the goal is to continue progressing, admitting your weaknesses so that you can deal with them is a strength.

Why aren't the people who are up in arms about abortion up in arms about war? Both are things no one really likes but accept as necessary.

True love is a struggle, like addiction. It's not something you can cross off your list as complete.

I love writers. I wanna suck the words from their mucus membranes and leave them speechless.

Though roads and people may take you far from where you started this life only the course of your actions will take you where you want to go.

Accept that you have no control ...but keep trying anyway.

An absence of negative qualities doesn't make someone a good person. It makes them bland.

It's a fine line between confidence and delusion.

Do yourself a favor and stay away from people who are too stupid to realize how far from smart they are.

You say that I'm a threat. Does danger make you wet? Do you haunt me because you're afraid that I'll forget?

Romance is the way you want what you can't touch and the way you touch what you can't hold.

Imagine going the rest of your life and never thinking about what you can get from anyone or what they can do for you, just appreciating them.

Often, the best thing you can do at any time is accept a gift, something you have no control over.

I ain't trying to go nowhere man. I'm just riding the wave.

All of my Snipple Snapples

You can't put an ocean back in the bottle.

I feel at home when I'm feeling out of place.

I'm one of a kind like everyone else.

Living takes its wage. We're all slaves. Some of us just live in a nicer cage.

If emotions are engines for actions them oceans gunna pass me by cuz I'm dead calm on some shit you can't classify.

No need to pick from a pool of ten when there's an ocean at your door.

Greed kills.

I pray to a god that lives inside thighs. Heaven is where I come from & every time I come back I die a little bit inside.

How much better off would we all be if we could see each other's souls before we saw each other's skin?

I'm not afraid of hell. I used to live in Arkansas.

If people had more sex they wouldn't be so pissed off about everything.

I haven't died yet but I plan to someday.

There's a billion people in the world that got it worse than you so nothing gives you the right to be an asshole.

The caged bird sings to god …right there in the cage with them.

The sachet of a passerby, her sweet perfume, all psychopharmacological. Her kind eyes, they pull you from the watering hole.

Coming to terms with reality is only the first toe stuck in an ocean of truth.

The realization that you're your own person is an emancipation not everyone learns to stroll through.

When you hunger for truth, positivity and negativity both taste like lies.

I'd rather not have sex with a hot annoying person than fuck them and have to listen to them talk for god knows how long.

You're probably not being as honest with yourself as you think you are.

My molecules on your molecules, running protons over skin, taking dust like a Valkyrie.

The less lines we draw between people make a bigger us and a lesser them.

Even monsters look pretty when they smile.

The fatal flaw in all philosophy is that humanity thinks they have the ability to grasp much of anything at all. The human experience is such a small teeny tiny fraction of life but it thinks it has the capability to grasp life's meaning.

When I see you checking every door to see which ones open, it looks to me like you're trying to steal shit.

If you knew what to look for you'd be amazed at what you could find.

Good people are lost in the carelessness. They're lost in the greed. They're lost in you thinking you matter more than them. Take the time to think. Please. We all need as many good people as the world can give us.

You live in the manner which you continue to create.

Better love than money.

All of my Snipple Snapples

Whenever I see girls drinking 80% of the time I see them, I can only assume that their genitals taste like a mouth full of pennies.

People tell you; be in love, be straight, be gay, be whoever you are but no one ever tells you it's ok to be single, it's ok to be alone. It's ok.

Fight hate with love. Be kind. Be generous. Be patient. Be friendly. Be open. Be courageous. Be joyous. Be happy. Be a protector and a giver and an encourager. Be your best you. Try.

You're trying to fit everything into your point of view but your point of view doesn't see everything.

The craziest thing humans do is think they're more important than any other speck of dust in an infinite dust storm.

Intelligence is not encouraged but the ability to understand, evaluate and apply is really the most useful life tool anyone can have.

What if animals took acid and could speak in human languages and when it wore off they had to go back to the old way and their lives were just weird from then on?

It's crazy that god has given us this great big world full of amazing things and people and beings and experiences and that we don't accept it all and appreciate each tiny little thing that makes all the big things so big.

Have you ever torn a world apart?

Acceptance is peace. Outrage is the key to change.

Our paradise in bed is lost every time we leave.

Wherever you go, whatever you do, someone's gunna try and give you shit for something. Fuck them. That's their shit. Don't take it.

A dog tired of being kicked stays away from swinging feet.

I'm just a cup trying to catch the ocean.

Leon McConnell

Atheists are people with no sense of smell insisting that smells don't exist.

Nothing can separate us from the love of God. Nothing said, nothing thought, nothing done. So don't ever think you're too far gone. God's always there.

The closer I get to money, the more comfort makes me uncomfortable.

When you cross the river of love by jumping from heart to heart, you only get to the other side by being heartless.

Who we are is more than DNA. We're written in ribbons of the spirit, all tied up between protein & antimatter.

You ever notice there's no Watts branch of Scientology?

Shout out to all the kids from nothing just trying to find their way in the world.

I want to communicate that I want to communicate less and less.

Being satisfied feels so strange.

There ought to be a rule of thumb dictating that no one topic ought to take up more than 20% of any given conversation.

If hamsters wrote their thoughts out for everyone to read, they'd still only be the thoughts of hamsters ...and only other rodents would care.

Have you ever noticed a recurring pattern of things that happen to you that are beyond your control but really inform and influence who you are? That's a design.

God is at the edge of every soul being the life between us all. I'm just trying to be open.

All of my Snipple Snapples

Love is filling every deficit, Accepting every wound, Making a canyon for every mountain And reading what's written in invisible ink.

Be your best you even when you don't feel like it, especially when you don't feel like it.

Those who lack drive are just along for the ride.

The most human thing about being human is accepting how much of your life is out of your control but trying to control it all anyway.

Even though a revolution is a circle, no one ever says they want a half a revolution.

Death sends ripples of imbalance through life's complicated equation and life shoots out in all directions against it, trying to keep the balance.

Every perfect moment must be paid for with a scar.

All the things I want in this world I can only get from myself.

I drink to feel dumb. Why do dumb people drink?

The people who are trying to not appear normal or boring are the normal and boring ones. The ones who are trying to come off as regular Joes, those are the freaks.

No animal lies the way humans do.

Every wrong you don't forgive turns bitter. Every drop of bitterness you hold onto is one less drop of happiness you can have. So it's in your own best interest to forgive everyone everything.

I don't want to have anything to do with people who hurt other people. I don't want to be anywhere around them.

There are corners in my mind crammed with memories, far too alive for the past they belong in.

Leon McConnell

If heaven is to be with god then realize that you don't need to die to be there.

Can you spread insomnia by not sleeping with people?

I'd bathe in the last shimmer of your dying star.

There's a lot to learn from people you find horribly annoying, like how to be less annoying.

You have no control over anyone else so don't make decisions in order to get something from them. Make decisions to get things from yourself.

Culture is just things people like ...and bacteria.

In the moment when all you have to do is reach out & take something but don't, know that someone else will and that it will never be yours.

In Los Angeles, most people can afford to live in Fresno.

There's no cure for being yourself. It's a double edged sword. Try not to cut your legs off.

Not even sleep is easy.

Following your heart is easy. It leaves a trail of blood.

It's crazy that people come from two different genitals, walk around for a while and then turn to dust.

Time is an ocean there's no point in fighting. Enjoy playing on its edges and do your best to sail across.

Some people are so blind, they look at a beautiful canyon and only see a scarred land.

It's not God I'm looking for. God isn't hiding. I'm looking to clean as many distractions from my own eyes as I can so that I can see God better.

All of my Snipple Snapples

Plenty of the worst decisions I've ever made are the best things to have ever happened to me.

So much of the trouble is being who you are surrounded by everyone else who's not.

It's crazy that everyone in the world was made by fucking ...except the test tube babies. They were made by jerking off for money.

I don't want to be anybody's anything. I just want to be yours.

Think of all the amazing things that happen that we don't appreciate because our genes have been programmed only to keep continuing.

You don't know what's waiting on the other side ...but honestly you don't know what's waiting for you on this side either.

Everyone's looking for their niche because without there being something you think makes you special you have to just accept that you're not special at all.

If you stop using chemicals to make you who you think you should be, you could just be who you are.

A speck of dust thinks success is becoming a piece of dirt.

If you feel the need to limit someone, it's probly because you're small.

Some bodies are the only world you'll ever know.

You don't learn what wet is by watching a body of water without ever getting inside.

If you're going to live your life to avoid pain you may as well resign yourself to the sofa. Pain is where you learn. Pain is when you grow.

Dreaming is the ghost of doing. That's why all your achievements are haunted.

What if dogs are making masterpiece art with pee and we just lack the sense to appreciate the beauty of it?

Leon McConnell

Sometimes you gotta wade through shit to get what you want.

Hard work entitles you to nothing but sweat.

We all want something we can touch …and hope is what we call it till we're holding it in our hand.

You ever notice that the people who want to make the world a better place are usually super fucking annoying?

Find your own way home.

When you want to do something grand & beautiful but aren't very creative, just destroy everything as best you can. Nothing is beautiful too.

All it takes for a dark light to turn bright is the flip of a switch.

I imagine heaven is a lot like Iceland, but warmer.

Defining myself by the past isn't going to help me move into the future.

I refuse to do a single thing to get anything from anyone without implicit communication and a fair exchange. Anything else is manipulation.

Personal development is not a group sport.

Props to everyone out there using all that god gave them …even if all god gave them is that ass and an iPhone.

When love comes take it. When pain comes take that too. Often they come close together. These are the things that make you human. Take it all.

Don't be afraid of time. Be aware of it. It's the one thing that stays the same.

Authority is only worth anything if you obey.

All of my Snipple Snapples

What if we just called people people and lost all the adjectives and learned to respect all beings? That'd be a good place to start.

It's fucking weird to lock up animals and stare at them while we eat churros.

I'm not expressing myself. I'm an express jet falling on deaf ears.

You'll never impress me with who you know or what you have. Impress me with who you are and what you do.

I don't know how smart it is but I always choose pain over compromise because I prefer freedom over comfort.

People are divided by their points of view. One person sees the leaves, another sees the trunk. Both argue over what a real tree looks like.

If God is all powerful then why do you insist on defending them?

All life stems from lust & All fulfillment from hunger.

There are three types of people in the world; those who make order of the chaos; those who make chaos in the order & those who just go with the flow.

Appetites are strange things. The more you feed them, the hungrier they get.

The key to success is a lot of fucking failure.

Want nothing from no one that you're not willing to give.

Fuck them. They can eat seven dicks.

You're not going to get ahead in life going the same way everyone else is. You're just gunna get in line.

Don't hope for heaven, build it.

Leon McConnell

Sex is the most innate & persistent reminder that you can't do everything by yourself.

Relationships are telling someone "te amo" when all they want is for you to say "I love you."

The things I thought I needed are now the knots that I'm untying.

When you're stabbing at greatness, first realize that it's not easy to catch, then learn to run faster and carry a sharper knife.

Sometimes I wish a moment of silence would last thirty years.

I wonder if the animals that do eat humans find the animals that don't eat humans annoying cuz they go around talking about it all the time.

If all your qualities are double edged, both good and bad, use them not to cut yourself down but to clear the path in front of you.

Humans are the weirdest animals.

Sentimentality stems from an inability to ascertain the sublime.

Sometimes you want to tell someone something but you don't have anything to say so you just let them slip away.

I just want to float on the surface of it all till something has enough gravity to suck me in.

Growing up in LA, I've always assumed I was either going to die by a cop or a car crash.

Problems are like cockroaches, get rid of one and there's 30 more you can't see just waiting to run through the kitchen.

If we looked at the world as a big heart we're all running through, there'd be a lot less blood spilt.

Love has no limits. You don't need to keep someone because you love them. They can walk away never to be seen again & you can love them all the same.

All of my Snipple Snapples

Beneath everything I've ever made, whether it's mediocre or amazing, is a pile of sacrifices, a mound of bodies I decided not to love enough.

Ours is a love of people passing. It only works because it's transitory. It's only beautiful because we happen into it so rarely.

People are blinded to the truth by what they want the truth to be.

Souls taste better with scars.

What a great gift it is to navigate being human.

The thin line between love and insanity is what you love loving you back.

It's crazy how some people want a friend so bad that they go out and make one with their genitals.

If you can't understand something, it can still matter but you'll never be able to know how much.

An artist by necessity must live an imbalanced life as the balance will always tip towards making beautiful things.

The world is going down and she's resting on my shoulder.

You go from a kiss on your mothers lips to one last kiss & sometimes we go years without.

You will come through the war of youth even keeled & proud of your scars into a post-apocalyptic maturity able to discern beauty between the greys.

Adoration, like any other substance of addiction, becomes tolerable and requires an upping in dosage which eventually leads to one's downfall.

The sun don't set & the sun don't rise. It's just the earth going in circles. Day and night are built on lies.

Leon McConnell

The thing I don't like about relationships is that starting them is easy but staying in them takes forever.

Life grinding you down may just be key to unlocking everything that lies ahead.

What you're asking for is a change. What you're yearning for is a transformation.

If you break my heart it's okay. It was probly too big anyway. Just don't break my face, no matter how much you want to. Then nobody will ever look at me the way I look at you.

Don't tell anyone what you know. Don't tell anyone what you've done. Don't tell anyone what you're not telling them.

Why be proud of where you're from? You just got pushed out of someone's vagina there.

A frayed quilt will unravel. A blanket folded in on itself stays warm.

Amongst clothes scattered along the sides of a freeway, were mittens my sister knitted for me when we lived in Yemen.

What's the point of being visible at all if the one person you want to see you won't look?

Try seeing more in people than whatever it is you want from them.

Sometimes when I say, "It's cool" what I actually mean is, "Don't worry about it. You're dead to me now anyway."

Even if you're only crawling by your teeth, continue moving forward.

Part 2:

1.
It's the unreasonable elements
People and moments
That don't fall into line efficiently
That give life its value
It's the things you're not guaranteed
That make anything worth having
It's the surprises
That make time worth enduring
It's the crazy homeless running naked
Guys selling tacos on the street
Socks on the train
It's a raccoon hissing from under your car
The Hollywood Hills on fire
Richard Ramirez three houses down
It's getting kidnapped in the desert
Deflecting whiskey bottles
Parents throw
It's an ex overdosing
Turning blue
And coming back to life
Demanding all night that you fuck her in the garden
It's the cops kicking in your door
Flashlights in your face
Grandma choking your little sister
It's an exorcism in the streets of South Gate
That cargo van driving by at 3 am
Right before you hear the gunfire
It's strangers inviting you to live in their basement
Handing you underwear
And asking you to help them wash their car
It's bullet holes in the people I love
Wondering if my dad's a serial killer
Ghosts floating through our family home
It's my childhood bulimia
The dolphins that dragged me through extinct lagoons
It's my knee cracking

Leon McConnell

In an unnamed celebrity's attic
That time I saw god
It's the hooker who smoked crack
In my lap when I was 17
And we were good friends
It's the train that dragged me
My week in prison
It's a hatchet I grabbed
A car I stole
The dirt I slept in
Drunken nights spent in strangers' mouthes
It's deciding not to die in Lake Michigan
Surfing atop a truck on the 105 interchange
That moment I transcended
When I was my best me
It's coughing up blood in India
Falling in love in the Arab Quarter
Walking through this labyrinth
It's beds soaked in waves
Walls drenched in screams
The violence you beg of me
It's being haunted
Xavier and I throwing roaches at each other
It's a game
It's when I burn the brightest
It's pants peed
Train tracks traveled
Bodies I memorized and loved
It's 6:15
The sun rising on the 710
It's all the secrets you'll never get
The smell of jasmine blooming on a sidewalk in Silverlake
It's the cusp
It's trust
It's the fact that I've been in 51 car crashes
It's bed bugs over and over
It's the slowing of my metabolism
The speeding up of time
The bending of my back

All of my Snipple Snapples

The fading of my eyes
The worry
It's being lonely
It's grasping onto strangers
It's letting everyone go
It's the current
Life
It's a tractor beam riptide rude awakening
It's mine
And it's over

    2.
Tell me a story. I can't sleep. Tell me something pretty and deep. Tell me I'm lucky that I can breathe. Tell me you love me and that you'll never leave
...cuz that's romance.

    3.
Every now and then I'll catch you under a street light fluttering
Pulled from the darkness of your home
By the voice of god in a candle
Echoing between aluminum cans
Mothing with me towards a dervished oblivion
Eyes bugged out
One foot off the diving board
Already launching into a lamp
Galaxies away
Sucking in the Divine wherever you can find it
Like we all do
Begging for an event horizon
Always on the cusp
You're radiating fireworks
Pheromoning carcinogens
Exhaling argon
And arclighting your eyes at me
Like I was a dream black ether
Not some paper doll cut out
Holding hands around a Christmas tree

Glimmering humanly
Wagging towards the light

    4.
To get something you have to spend something
If you get something without paying for it
Someone else paid
It's a gift
If you receive gifts but do not give them
You will be imbalanced
An imbalance always leads to action
Action creates or takes life
Balance will always find a way
Better to drive the balance than be driven
Better to give than to receive

    5.
Why not take a city of pressed bare flesh
And call it base camp beneath the mountain
Let it shame tip tops and lonely climbers
With rich oxygen bags of blood that slosh in dance
Towards tents of heavy meals
Covering unpacked picks and rappelling ropes
Frostbite wants your body parts
And you call that evolution
Becoming cold blooded?
Oh what a backwards humanity

    6.
When you're in love or infatuated or even just fucking someone else, your universe is that much bigger. It goes from being just you in your head to another person's smile and thoughts, their warm body and dislikes. Connecting with other people makes our worlds explode with possibility.

    7.
I've been drifting along for years
Away from the mainland
The islands I step aboard getting smaller and smaller

All of my Snipple Snapples

As I pass this continental shelf, keeping look out for the next archipelago
It occurs to me that maybe I should stop drifting
Maybe I'm just afraid
Maybe I should dive in

8.
You're a toothache I'm attached to, my tongue runneth over
It might be pain but nothing makes me feel like this

9.
Any monster, any abyss swallowing you whole
Doesn't expect you to caress its insides on your way down
But dreams of a loving touch with every bite

10.
If you're looking for an oasis
For a paradise
Or a spot of shade and a bit of rest
Just climb the closest wall
Hop the fence and scurry over
Find pleasure in what you can find
And jump every wall along the way

11.
Drenched in dark sweat
I clench my teeth
And spit
Raise the shovel again
It's not cold in here
That furnace blazes so damn hot
I can touch fire with my fingertips
And you wouldn't feel me
I'm frustrated with my lack of money
It's too big
It doesn't fit in my lifespan
I grow bitter
All night long we shovel
Jimmy & Me

Leon McConnell

This habit of being poor
I'm afraid will make nothing of me
And nothing of Jimmy
Dearest Rebecca
I see the water on the windows outside
And I wonder if this is what hell is like
We've lost hope
I don't want to die pity
Love Al
Please send me bread

12.
ime a note in a smoky room
a thought in miles davis placenta
all this fog
this is my planet
and all the people drinking their glasses of water
scheming about sex & money
my life is a background to them
outer space is a wooden room
my life is in yure ears
quicker than a mayfly
i burn out like eyelash transmissions
when the alto sax flashbulbs this into yure memory
they call me greensleeves
next thing you know ime a universe
cool raises altars to me in the fresh of life
where their head is space to a smoky room
and in every step ime reincarnated
imagination & the trombone i come from is a blackhole
nod to my infinity
nirvana's just a toe tap away

13.
there aren't any children in my neck of the woods
in my part of the city
not that anyone around here'd make some
i could see us sending our son out for milk
past the winos, the sex shops and the needles in the street

All of my Snipple Snapples

he'd come back drunk with an aching asshole
and a shot to ease the pain
pleasure has a big huge palace on my block
where her people come to worship
she doesn't clean up
she rages all night long
and every adult in this city has given their children up to god
to be burned for water
on the fire of their blazing loins

14.
there comes a time
when your ideals can't support you
and you question
everything you ever thought
or ever did
all you want is to find a corner
to curl up in
so you don't have to face the world
you thought you lived in
the ways you thought you understood
when this time comes
you just live
that's the way things go

15.
the dogs that communication run
foam their mouthes
at my syntax flesh
and carry paragraphs to evil
from hills of my mind
they feed the system
with assonance
fueling digestive juices
so machines conspire against me

Leon McConnell

16.
The Three Signs of Civilization

Nike
McDonalds
Coca-Cola

17.
one pitch black somewhere
outside the little box
a bag of marbles fell right in
then started spinning
until they stopped

18.
I never think of Hollywood as collagen injections
I always think of Hollywood as homeless people with no shoes
Making forts in upturned shopping carts and shitting in the bushes
It's funny that people want to end homelessness
Because I want to end greed
They're kind of opposites on the seesaw
Except greed would make more homeless because it can't stand
That anyone who doesn't have would exist in spite of its always wanting more
While homeless people I'm pretty sure
Don't really give a fuck if you get collagen injections

19.
Along with the waves of tossed cars coming from going
I thought I heard an alarm out my window
Somewhere by the rail yard
In the valley between here and Lincoln Heights
But when I stopped to listen
Along with brake pads deep past their use by date
Screeching through midnight on the 10
I realized it was nightingales
And bats
And the soft paws of a coyoht

All of my Snipple Snapples

Passing by shanties on the fire road
It was the blue of cancer season's hushed slumber
It was a cool sheet
An ant passing between our bodies
Looking me in the eye
It was a calm insomnia
The memory of a ghost that's gone now
And my internal clock ticking away the seconds till I actually have to be awake

   20.
I imagine sometimes hell seeps into this world the way mental illness drifts through downtown up from skid row, threatening to come back with a crowbar if you don't give it a job while it stands there mammering at you, holding out a cigar box, the lid turned up, with its resume written in schizophrenic crayon jarble.

   21.
Some people call surrender a warm red bath. I think of it as the total acceptance that you will not succeed. Nor will you be remembered or amount to anything of note. People surrender every day. I don't think I'm ready for that. Life is this immense fucking mountain and I refuse to make a camp and settle in. I'll keep on sinking my claws into the rock face and scaling the Matterhorn inch by inch, year by year till my body is broken and my soul crawls out of it into the wind, blown away.

   22.
When you're friends with monsters
You think more about them smiling
And less about the blood on their teeth

   23.
Want is the root of all suffering
Try wanting less
If you want something
Make sure it's something you can get by yourself
If you need something from someone
Give them something of equal value in return
If you take more than you give

Leon McConnell

You want too much

    24.
    Adrift on charity
    All my efforts put in carelessly
    I erred on the side of trying to find
    A balance in sincerity
    But only found an ocean I can float on
    And I don't know if these deep waters
    Offer any clarity

    25.
There is no poetry to youth. but people are always amazed when you cross a blind kitten with a raging bull, so we glamourize smooth newborn rubber balls straight out the muck ...faces with no cracks that barely know life.

But I don't mind a couple cracks here & there. I think they look better with a little dirt rubbed in 'em, if only to show the persistency of dirt or the flippancy of cracks. I think when a woman gets older, she looks better. The dirt's set in. The cracks are subtle & obvious & not looming over her like mythological question marks. I don't mind 'em dirty or cracked or slightly broken.

I find cheating perfection to be a high art form and an imperfection a piece of art; a wrinkle, some cellulite, a little flab here and there, the balance a body toys with between gross and eye pleasing or tasty to touch. Perhaps a ruddy complexion has filled in with twenty years' time and her face plays like memories from the jukebox as your fingers go over around & round.

It's beautiful that beneath tiny inclinations ...a collection of perhapses, is the mind which goes on. I find a will that stands against dirt, which only seeks to drive us back into the ground, incredibly sexy. The long drawn out chess game of the body, the sand, the wind, the rain, the cliffs, the rivers, the whole weather of it all that a woman wears through middle age, till nothing can take care of her ...these years are flutteringly erotic.

26.
down here in the southern hemisphere
the lonely bats crawl between sundown and dark up
like blind beggar mice pulling themselves by their two front feet
across the desert of sky slipping into senility
flapping at the pink with a darkness
till the last from their tribe disappears
and we call the night complete

27.
eyh memorize steps through dark houses
write on white pages
touch uncaressable lips
perspirate bead drops
leave traces wiped across memory
stains of royal hatred
ink bludgeonings
velvet skin eye trains
gliding across my sheet leaf corporeal
can you read me?

28.
in your lap is the warmest pillow
when my eyes sting
and my mouth's caked in blood
i go to sleep there
in your mouth is the sweetest pill
you must be a nurse
you must be a garden
my fingers butterfly your milkweed skin
eyhma dragon
a simple slug
nothing yuhre tongue would want to be like
yuhre body is the god that formed me
the sun i grasp at
yuhre eyes are caring saints
you look at me sustenance and laughter

Leon McConnell

children carrying warm gifts
you must be life & round
a mother
you must be earth in spring
you must be a teddy bear hanging from my hand
you lay in my arms just like i lay in yours
i know peace with you
cry stain prison bars across my face
grow when yuve gone
trapped in time away
yuhre hands are a rabbit hole
a dream ive fallen into
yuhre sleep is the quiet blanket of a universe
yuhre days end a sky covered in pacifity

29.
If rain were a cloud falling to its knees upon a body of water
Making ripples by its mere approaching
Till the air between them was 100% humidity
Till every splash was a kiss not given hard enough
And every wave flung towards the sky
A finger floating gently towards the nimbus
Then maybe You & I wouldn't be so thirsty for each other
Then maybe drowning wouldn't be such a bad thing

30.
gauze green bandages of a bikini
cover her wilted sick milk skins
a dirty band aid seeped in vagina
day glows its way across disease
oozing an ocean of infection
tall & gangly, her skin is full of broken pieces
slushing in the sand
they're gunna have to cut her off just to save her
amputate that skinny girl off this planet

All of my Snipple Snapples

31.

The world is going back to spirits. Millenia ago we would meet demons and demigods in secret places and beg for blessings to find our way. Humans tossed the gods aside and worshipped idols of their own invention; iron, steam, electricity, industrial technology, circuits and clouds ...a collective consciousness. Together we realize that we've been making the wrong road and are working our way back to transcending, talking to ghosts, walking through the borderlands between worlds and realizing that skin is shallow. God is talking to whoever's listening, asking you to come ashore across deep waters. This is our rebirth.

32.
tilt my head back for the bottle
keep it quiet because the voices in my head don't like the competition
turn the lights off because the darkness in my soul
could use some company
and drink to vomit out that aching in my stomach

33.
you were the days of a fork in the road
of a public telephone on the sidewalk
i sat with quarters in hand
and called out so long distance
you were the days of decisions made
beds i slept in
a dream ive savoured
you were a girl
memories of a grail
ingrained in grains
of a time we never had

you rolled by like quarters downhill
past my fork in the road
where i sat feet dangling off the curb
against a pay phone
over sidewalks so long distance
you were days away light speed
a telephone voice in a dream i savoured

beds i slept in
some mess i made
while the girl
memories of a grail
ingrained in grains
of a time we never had
slipped through ourglass
and grew
deserts across america
nowadays
i get so thirsty for
oasis

34.
Every once in a while
The piece of me people call a soul
Should be drowning
It takes a wreck of shivers
Six feet beneath the surface
And dies for I dunno
Twenty minutes or so
Cold water in and out
Icicles dangling off my lung leaves
Wallowing in death warms me
This nap of being is a rescue boat
All the ocean ghosts and I
Follow the parachute flair under alien stars
Treading water back to life

35.
Where I work at the meat plant
I can see the tiny lights from the hills of East L.A.
It's quiet, even with the factory
The ear plugs have nothing to do with it
Just like a hard hat doesn't keep me from thinking
The sheer depopulous of an industry town
pushes a finger over the lips of night
It covers those with a blanket hush who cannot sleep
I look forward to sunrise over the riverbed

All of my Snipple Snapples

A red dawn from the freeway overpass
Till then I wear my iron jumpsuit
Content with the night like a figure in a dream
who needs it to exist

36.
I wrapped my muse in a blanket
Like childhood beneath the night sky
And kissed her lash like sunshine
Stabbing through dreams
To press reset against flesh

37.
You can never truly know a person
You can only follow the threads to their big ball of string
And unravel while they speak to you in a dead language

38.
always chase god
and butterflies

39.
There's no us vs them
Stop dividing us into factions
Do you know what the world would be
If we realized the extent of our control
Is limited solely to our actions
There'd be peace

40.
firewood
smells like childhood
on christmas day
next to the fireplace
by the christmas tree
and all these presents are just for me

Leon McConnell

41.
how concentryte are the thoughts
which kick in genius
that the sog in mind pick up
from the bottom of their shoe
whence they've trickled down
from how beyond our understanding

42.
writing with a razorblade
chewing on a middle finger
wondering where i put my gun
back to the wall
above the blankets
in my bedroom
dreaming about the riverbed
remember when i went ice skating
the only light flickers
like gas lamps
from beneath my eyelids
and it reminds me of a birthday cake
mom's calling from the living room
up the stairs
over the vacuum
in her apron
with her hair down
black chrysler in the driveway
night on night
hiding bloodstained tires
and red flecked rims
broken speakers echo countless searches through time and hunger
they don't make music for me
the devil roams the earth like a hungry lion
looking for whom he may devour next
he just wants things his way
i can understand that
it's not so crazy
it's crazy not to want things yure way
and crazy to believe that they are

but not crazy to try or pretend
dinner's ready
bandage wrap the forearms
descend into the carpet
shadows of hooded sweatshirts
white teeth and beard stubble
empty my pockets of poems
written on tiny packets of sugar
front & back
take the fuck you
out of fingers
and bury it deep inside my heart
where i put that world ive been carving
to fit a homeostasis
and hold this soul ime bursting
macaroni & cheese

43.
I make dog food
I work in the meat plant at the grinders
My favorite place is the thaw room
It's this big warehouse with five or six air conditioners
the size of diesel trucks
You gotta keep the meat cold
The thaw room has like sixty racks full of frozen meat
four stories high
Thirty one tanks of pumpable meat
A chunky milk shake like substance that flows
out of a pipe organ next to my computer
And four tanks of blood
Each tank holds twenty thousand kilos
But I like the thaw room cuz it's cold
I need the cold to breathe
It might be all in my head
But it's not like I spill my guts about this everyday
So I doubt that anyone thinks I'm crazy
The smell doesn't bother me
The thaw room has all these catwalks behind the blood tanks
I like to lay there and just chill in the cold

Leon McConnell

where no one can see me
In a dark corner
It's peaceful
I feel like I'm escaping to my own place
I only get a little scared sometimes because of the ghost
I haven't seen the ghost
But I feel like I feel the ghost when I'm walking around
Some people say they've seen him
But if I did I wouldn't tell anyone
Cuz people might think I'm crazy
That's why I keep my eyes closed
I get a sore throat from the cold
But I don't mind
It's hot out there
I don't have any place of my own
The world is folding me up and crushing
I'm lucky for the big open spaces
I'll take them how I can get 'em
Nobody knows I stay there
I don't tell anyone
It's where I keep my sanity
Safe

44.
People amaze me. Knowing them is my treasure. I collect them, grabbing them by shoulders and lips around every corner, never spending a single soul. Letting the money run through my fingers and walk right out my life. Wherever I turn brings the opportunity to open one up and inhale them, really let them breathe, let them ramble, learn their hows and whys, appreciate the time it took to carve them, savour their intangibles, the wholes greater than their sums.

Some you learn in ways no one else ever will. Some only get to be that them they are because you're you and it brings this all out, a perfect combination where the treasure treasures the treasurer, where we treasure the we we've made of each other. That's real humanity.

All of my Snipple Snapples

I pray I can be counted amongst those who share their clean, their quiet, their safe, their home, their food, their car, their time, their touch, their joy, their peace, their fire and I pray I not take more than I give.

45.
Dead greed polymorphous heart box insides void of hope
Hollow echoing one thought lonely in solidarity
Solitary confinement in skin under open skies
Buried deep into society

46.
After the party is adventures through the mundane
You accept what is, having mulled over it all
Your body tired, breaking down fat and slow
This is how death comes. It's natural.
There are no more mountain tops.
There's kittens
And the unexpected side of repetition.

47.
A person is not the fat hanging over their jeans
Or the nose that hates you stinking of smoke
A person is the electricity coursing through
A million thoughts in a red sweater
In 182 pounds of 65 year old bone and meat
That loves movies and rain
And sent a volt through you
The first time it touched
One day that electricity will be unplugged
And you can never switch that person on again

48.
It's only here, folded in these pages that I could ever tell anyone that sometimes I'm walking down a rainy street in Reykjavik while the next moment I'm floating off the shores of Ometepe or sitting on a sandbar in Glenelg drifting down Las Vegas Boulevard New Year's Eve like time and place were nothing. I feel so lucky, so gifted, so amazingly blessed.

49.
Cuddled against grandma's fat shoulders
I don't think human is the most complex machine
Her gardenia perfume pulls reason over my eyelids
Crafting a dark inside contention
The old woman starts to snore
As I board an oatmeal cookie memory
...and rail off into sleep

50.
the days i hung like spanish moss languidly
from your shoulders crashed
great walls of virus rose mountain high
tumbling sunshine pink lemonade down broken glass
now i live recklessly
burned the whole forest down
tied a brick to the gas pedal and set off for desert body roads
dust hungry children underfoot
dreaming of you in a swamp
hanging from a tree of your own

51.
our souls have bodies
whole worlds that rub off on lips
minds get lost, thought by thought
stolen by lovers, trapped in an embrace

our chain link valve heart lips murmur
hematoma tangled praises
tiny red songs of a constant
thank you

52.
smoke hangs from your clothes by its memories
imagining your touch in lipstick
a collar, a pink embrace
your incendiary appetite clasping fetish models
white, thin and longing…

heart burning purposefully towards a kiss
every ash scorned oscillates in an aggravated state
love is haunted and it screams
wishing you cancer from hell
spewing affection's ectoplasm
wrinkle deep, virginia slim cum trails
blown across your finger
wedding you with this ring
in a puffy caress

53.
in the dark clarity of quiet pm's
another day subsides to the bedroom
the whir of ceiling fans
a breath & sniffle filling its ear
a man chiseled in the doorway
sweat and denim clinging to his skin
stares at an empty bed
and ingests peace by the senseful
...exhales this moment through a pen

54.
i wrote this on your window
but it faded away when i stopped breathing
it said i'm watching you
and a smiley face
actually carrying more in subtext between lines
than real abc letters
like you look like a puppy dreaming
when your feet kick
the way they have little doggy dreams
and it's cold out here
there's boot scruff smile stitches
kicked across the chin of your door
i smile back
and wonder who stitched them
fucktakeadeepbreath
the box cutter in my pocket
reminds me why i'm here

Leon McConnell

i got you a present
what are you dreaming of?
you look pretty when you sleep
wake up and breathe on me
xxwifey
happy birthday

55.
between the cracks of my lips
sandstorms have weathered ravines
deep pink to the blood passages
writ & drawn from the finger of god
holy implicit scrawlings
left on flesh like commandments
smoothed glyphs to run your teeth over
played like a music box
transposed in a telegraph
spiders with violins
waltzing tightropes up your nerves
read me when i kiss you
an open book that makes you shudder

56.
All day long my life shakes with a manic hunger that nothing fills but the impression of god. God I feel in inhalation. God halfway up behind my ears. God I cannot eat nor understand. There's a few ticks of true real peace that bare a memory, a photo to think about and wear. These are the boundaries. Oceans infringe all through me. I can never cross them. God is there. So easy to come to. He floats on by. I want to drink him in. I'm too incapable of drowning. Far too incapable.

All of my Snipple Snapples

57.

Dear Sari,

I was just thinking a lot of things and I can't talk or type fast enough to get them down but I'll try anyway. I was thinking I wish I could be someone you'd like to get to know over and over again and I know you'll say that I haven't been listening or that I don't understand you because that's not the point.

The point is that you need more. I'd like to be that nonetheless because I don't want to be appreciated by more than one person. One person is enough. It means you're appreciated but then when you're not appreciated by the one person, it means you're not appreciated at all thus depreciating your integral value and it sucks to feel worthless.

Then I got to thinking of several other things that I'm currently capable of recalling. One was the first time I met Nick and Matt. I said that I had no time for interesting people and the reason for that is I really do just not want to be(period) The effort of being interesting falls so short of the grand scale of what's possible and any intention of taking up the space of an interesting person is defining yourself, saying this is who I am. This is what I've settled for, impressing you with my character traits. So, I want no character traits because I don't want to impress anyone because I don't want to be less than what's possible. This makes me think that I expect too much from people and life. It also makes me think of something I wrote in a story about this girl who had this vast personality but didn't find any point in it and hated people who had so little self-control that they had to be themselves all the time and I got really mad at you about that once, that you always had to be you and couldn't just ever let it go.

Maybe I'm really messed up. No one in the world will tell you this is a good way to be and I guess now it's been proven to me but try as I might this whole system of thinking is etched into my fucking core. Sometimes, I wish I could function on water, sex, and fast cars alone. I might be really happy. Those three things excite me but I feel gross for even putting that statement down as it's a pinpoint for personality and I don't want you to ever think that's who I am. Perhaps I've

Leon McConnell

carried this off so well, that you think I'm nothing I ever was and anytime I feel like being the person I always have been, I've thought myself too far deep into the corner and that that person is gone. I am what I thought I should be. I hate all this philexisto babble.

You should have met me when I was 17. I would have loved to impress you. I would have made you laugh till you peed your pants as I'd done to girls on the street and small children but I would have walked away as soon as you batted an eyelid.

I was also thinking about this Jack Kerouac book, The Dharma Bums. I hate his bifbammbooisms and how full of himself and his hipster/buddha/wino friends and lifestyle he is, but there's like just 2 or 3 little things in there that make the whole book worthwhile. One is what I was telling you about, how pretty girls make graves. And the other is this, "Everyone knows everything."

I think about that sometimes. Do we really all get it all and just pick and choose what we decide to ignore or follow based on personal preference? It seems like that sometimes. The way we've lived our lives, this isn't how I wanted to live my life. I've just had such a hard time trying to fit what you want with what I want and pull it all off. It was just so easy to be happy without actually accomplishing anything.

Life is funny. It wasn't what I wanted and it wasn't what you wanted. It's just what we did. I was so run down and fatigued, swimming uphill. In a way I admire you for doing something you wanted. It's just that, if I was gunna do that, I would have taken care of you as well. I actually thought about leaving you several times because you can be a very difficult person to get along with. I just thought it would be stupid for our whole time to not come to some sort of fruition where maybe a lot of the things I thought were a source of trouble wouldn't be there which is why I wanted the month, a sort of maybe.

So I don't know what I'm gunna do now. Nothing seems very important.
    xxLeon

All of my Snipple Snapples

    58.
chill blows a kiss under the doorway
that crawls on graven fingernails
towards freesia in the windowsill
creeping at the pulse of spanish candles
whispering death in cold horns to all matadors
orange light like blood
splashes against the wall from red curtains
a sea across the floor
dragged along the beach
cold's kiss sits well in my heart
it's lips are goose bumps
that dark sweeps away with warm fingers
stray lashes fallen like answers from heaven
god breathing down no no no
close your eyes and cancel your prayers
let every saint shiver
let every fire die in the snow
oh lucifer damned in icicles
stop the sun from rising
stop sneaking into my room

    59.
dark keeps warm blindly weaving
spinning hours at the loom
while white stares at white
black is held together in a blanket
harboring no dreams of corona fingers
caressing her ragged luna
no particle waves soft like feathers
down an old scarred cheek
no bed of lovers embracing in an eclipse
our blind seamstress toils in silence
shunning explosions of recognance
detesting daybreak & its robbery
abhorring the fuller spectrum
so arrogant
dark works for no love songs

no children at picnics who run & play
her gift gets discarded every morning
her door closed by a so called center of the galaxy
kicking her to the curb like some cheap fill in
but dark matters
i see her every time i close my eyes
she's in my soul
in every thought
and this long gestation
this endless abortion
one way or another has to end

60.
la is golden narcotic castles
ohmygod morphine puddles mexicans built beaches in
bus rides from whittier to malibu with the top down
orgasming off sunshine
i take smog straight from the needle
my life is a hazeglassy eyes and slow days
angels on my cell phone
talking about how chhh wants to whisper in my ear
something under bridges chhhh static
run like static rivers chhhhhh rabbits
doses of god are given out weakly
diluted every sunday on venice sidewalks
in exchange for prayers between palm trees
children fuck in orange sunsets with their windows open
the ocean swallows their two story moans
dreaming of the day
waves drown the sound of traffic

61.
scratchy caffeine eyelids
dragging lashes across lenses like icy lakes
cracked & covered over
sleep dead beneath the water
its last breath foggy particles
spirits gnawing at the ether
frost bit awake till hell freezes over

All of my Snipple Snapples

god a fucking nap'd be dreamy
heaven is a subconscious
crusty tear ducts running slobber
drowning pillow clouds
snowmen stacked in feathers
up to my eyebrows
whispering happy wishes
carved in marshmallows
eskimo kissing me blissfully
till i blow the sun out of every iris i can open
and melt this motherfucker
damn i need some fucking sleep
now

62.
A deep cut can remind you that you're real, that you're human. When you're disconnected, seeing blood connects you to a body. This body is you. This blood means you're living. Every living thing has a body just like you. You're part of everybody. If one body questions its being, it's bound to be that many if not most if not all's question too. Every body bleeds. Every body questions. You're in there. You're one surrounded by many. See, you're connected. Just don't bleed to death.

When you run out of blood, i.e. it all falls out, the body won't work. They have to throw it away. If you are anywhere you're not alive. You're nobody. Nobodies cannot be connected by their very nature. They have no body parts to connect. You are permanently disconnected. Even the clouds, mere vapor, are physical droplets of H20 gathered into groups. When you're no body, not even air, you have no breath. You can't ask for help. You've gotta find your own way now.

63.
mankind is a field
grown of cynical seed
that blows whichever way the world turns him
his soul is negativity and requires wisdom like a light
that sparks this field
& is pushed forward by the wind

fuel becomes understanding
as the dim men grass char coal
and pass the fire
the vehicle which drives through them

64.
i live in mecca by the scientology building
kids with bad haircuts come in droves to dance on my block
worship in my neighborhood
prayers are uttered in shitty dance moves
dignity sacrificed in ritual flirtation
exhaustion promises ecstasy
turns to alcohol and wishes for cocaine
outside the temple incense burns wrapped in bacon
you can smell meals running down the block
street vendors pushing grills on wheels from cops
their sausage still grizzling
children bow down and worship all bodies
because bodies provide
no one goes hungry home alone ungroped in dark corners
these fingers bring tidings of great joy
god shines through damaged eardrums
every night of the week
everybody loves him and his prophets are always stoned
here in mecca someday we'll dance together
we'll kneel & pray
then drift bedward heavenwise
into the rising sun

65.
windows hushed open away from mada's bedroom
you shhhhshhhd me but i knew to be quiet
nothing stirred, only you and i
the roses were sleeping
thorns stood watch over them with samurai swords
bleeding you, trampling through hallways of rose beds
we snuck in through your window
and i fell in love with the dark
we kissed and fucked and laughed very quietly

All of my Snipple Snapples

    i had to go to the bathroom but i peed into a cup instead
    i couldn't find my clothes
    the morning stirred around us
    the sun rose and i closed my eyes naked against your back
    sighing smilely
    your bed was murder to my pain
    your stiff colored hair tussled on my shoulder
    like dreams our souls were whisked away with daybreak
    and i fell in love with the dark

    water in little rainlets parachutes with warm intentions to hot skin
    taking a long ride down every inch of your body
    like my fingers, like my lips, like this
    i like this a lot
    you looked like a life commercial
    selling me showers, skylights, sunshine, rocks,
    and half bodies trying to conform
    somethings can only be bought with bites and kisses, like you
    newborn, glowing, translucent
    good lord
    kiss, shudder, and close my eyes
    i want to buy it
    i want to buy it all

    and the last line should read
    I pray to god every single light breaks

    66.
    think of any black space anywhere
    and there i am, a thought just like you
    the two of us in your head
    you can keep your eyes closed and still see me
    you can keep your mouth with just us in it
    quiet, cuz that's how black spaces like it best
    as you lay looking ime looking back
    see me black

67.
American Greed
The little black & white television set
Hanging from her cabinets over a toaster
Just screams poverty
2 inch screen 3 inch screen
Maybe 4 inches
Discarded cans of Coca-Cola
Feminine product tampon napkin boxes in the trash
Acne. The round edged brown lettuce
Scented frigerator with Cadillac writing
Fridgedaire or something like that
An emblazoned poverty
Her stringy hair
This television ad for television youthes
With pretty faces forces alienation
Upon its viewers and cracks dreams
Desperate attempts at convincing

Kind fat women go unforgotten
We pay homage to them here
In Mother's Day cards
Wonder how they ever breed
Her ice cream melted, slob
Bleaching lecherous sunshine
Sinking away black & white tiles
In the kitchen tide
Drowning America in pools of light
Vermin gather, tending her funeral
Sit upon her dinner suited
Catfood catpiss hair
Unbitten feeding hands missed
Meow, Saluted
I call that dying with nothing

68.
an honor to steal
that i would want it so much
that books should be sold
just so men could be honored

69.
artists should take to writing on walls
words they want read
instead of hiding them on leafs
in trees that fall
only in fires

70.
on avalon
when the casino wheel stops spinning
and champagne glasses are dead to the floor
the ferry captain starts his engine
he gets up at four every morning
children playing in the parking lot
come soon through to high school
where we stopped in an old camaro
to play on the slide at the park
and talk to local miscreants
who have no liquor store to curb their tendencies
and bullshit about bullshit
oh buffaloes and boars and the cliffs of the island
are invisible from the naval station
before the bridge to sunset beach
all i can see are the mountains of catalina
and this dream of going away

71.
cockroaches come out of my dresser drawers
out of my monitor across my mouse pad
they dance all night inside my microwave
there's so many of them
they don't really bother me

none of em try and take my things
but sometimes i just feel like being alone
and they walk all over like they own the place
my name's on the lease
i don't kill them
most of em aren't afraid of me
but if they get too close
i probly flick them away
i need my personal space
and they don't understand that
that is what i least admire about my roaches
their lack of listening skills
and just how insensitive they can be
besides that they're okay
as long as they stay out of my bed at night

72.
When your soul aches
Does it make you a better person
And when you smile
Does that mean you forgot you've been hurten
When you tell someone everything that's inside
But don't tell them everything
Does that mean that you lied
Can you kiss till you fall in love
Is it a hole with a bottom
How do you know when you get there
Is that when it hurts
How long does it take to get out of
Would you live in a hole with me
Would you float above the bottom and promise to never leave
Are we all our lists of questions
Are yours the same as mine

73.
I would like to be perfect
But then I wouldn't be me
And that's insincere
So I overplay my lesser qualities

All of my Snipple Snapples

>Because it's easier
>And they're there
>
>74.
>ovulating like a time bomb
>another biological weapon
>in stiletto heels she walks the subway
> !!!!!!terrorist alert!!!!!!!!
>
>75.
>birth saw me in mud & trees
>i ate from the ground
>and talked to god
>my childhood was spent learning
>sometimes dull to understand
>nonetheless i wrote it all down
>each word a building block
>i carved cities from the husks of idiocy
>my children walked their steps
>played on my slow ideas
>tore limbs from thoughts
>and stirred their own understanding
>their minds were steel
>hot & ready to be poured
>piled up
>they made nations
>built ships
>we took to the water when it was pure
>i spoke with whales and sang
>my heart screamed
>my body fell
>all my babies
>we're more than animals
>our graves are living
>each electric impulse
>inscribed on microorganisms
>germs nanotechnology
>our failures are reassembling wrong
>slowly walking up to god

on stairs of death
fashioned like evolution
from whatever we can take
one day ile be more than this
realer than ascension
awake from dreaming
one day ile be knocking on yure door
carrying a universe
ready to step in

76.
if i had one thing to say
one thing to tell someone
utter meaning
pure truth
unadulterated
an enzyme
a spark
something
they could take hold of
and run with
something to spin the world straight
id keep it to myself
and let people pay
close attention

77.
when heaven fell all savage and burning
reeking of ozone and charred cumulus
it didn't really change much. people adapt
dead angels littered the streets like split tires
we just drove around em
people need to get places y'know
some folks were worried
"what's this mean for the afterlife?"
"why fucking bother?"
churches became black holes ...like evil
catholics were pissed. mormons took to looting
but i mean ...besides that, shit was status quo

All of my Snipple Snapples

there was like ...an effort to send aid
but nobody knew what was needed exactly
dead souls crowded the public parks and movie theaters
what do they eat?
eventually it got so that i wouldn't leave my house
i couldn't say no to all those cherubs holding signs
begging for love or money
they're just............beautiful
i was going broke, depleted
anyway, i like it in my house
no one watching over me
heaven at my feet, wings in the gutter
it don't feel like hell that much at all
not even a little bit

78.
the wish factory smells like fabric softener and ramen noodles
hovel apartments honeycomb hollywood
housing sad lonely unemployed entertainers
their laundry hangs from clothesline bodies
their souls leak down windowsill faces
and haunt liquor store aisles fogging up the freezer glass
i let em die every day on my way to the subterranean
step over puddles of wisher wells washing in the gutter
brushing their teeth with grey goose
breakfast clamped to hope's nipple
starving cuz that bitch died
sucking the blood from society
till their veins dry
tied off with an apron at a casting call
one last sigh till euphoria
and heaven takes em
 then you just die

79.
when you're lost, consumed, absorbed
fully gone and unconscious of anything
except what has you
it's hard to imagine there's an outside

hard to believe in a fuller fulfilling
it's like the entire act of living is mined
endured for these momentous gems
they're not something you can carry around
people atmosphere an aire of zircon memories
a glimmer like bottlecaps in golden years
memories of treasure are worse than worthless
they're a weight
a gravity to the grave
and so yule die in desert memories
stuck in time like a pharaoh in sand

80.
If you can stand waiting
Time will take you away
Why cling to a moment
When every moment has a revolution
Your childhood on the cusp
Doesn't deserve a haunting
Your world spinning
A song on the record player
Sufis encircling their god
This whole solar system
A lazy Susan
Raindrops rippling in a puddle
If you can stand waiting
Time will take you away

81.
it's gotta be horrible for god
god, the one & true god
the only real god
he must be lonely
there's billions of people praying to him
asking for this, forgiveness for that
never, i brought you roses
let's hold hands and walk through the garden
so they don't really know him
so it's gotta be lonely

All of my Snipple Snapples

    i mean
    he threw this big party
    paid for it all
    decorated, made the food
    nobody brings a present
    nobody gives him a kiss
    no one really cares
    mankind has invested so much in itself
    takes such pride in advancements
    and such pain in the savagery
    when we're just a puppy, god's best friend
    to love God
    to really love God, out of pity
    out of thanks, out of knowledge
    from your heart, with a single thing that you do
    is as natural as gravity
    with nothing holding you down
    imagine flying straight into heaven
    and having to face a god
    you don't love

    82.
When you kill yourself, you put a black hole down in the middle of your family and friends. The closer anyone is to you the more things suck for them. Gravity pulls all the way out to your acquaintances, people you knew from school, friends of friends of friends.

I have a lot of gravity pulling on me. Some people can fly. They never look at their life and think of outer space. They're lucky but I'm stronger from fighting the pull all my life. When I've gotten passed the event horizon, I hulk my way through shit. These black marks make me indestructible.

One day probly the entire universe will shadow over, gone through some rabbit hole. Then we'll all be bulletproof.

83.
I have a sense of doom coming, this small black thing in the corner of the room. All the fight we've been through, the mountains we climbed on our hands and knees are not an escape. Peace is a lull, a deep breath. Doom is waiting, hurt by our hope, cut by relief. Our relative calm and subtle joys are an icepick in our parents' heart. Like an avalanche, "you are mine" starts as a snowball in the face thrown far away, tumbling deep deep deep. And this thought echoes through the valley while doom crawls after us, till even darkness is haunted, till a poltergeist flails at every fragment of this malevolence personified. We've settled. We're stable. Doom has had time to catch up. We think we're safe in our kitchens, the sturdiest warren in Hiroshima. I never even heard a knock on the door.

84.
My smile is a beach but my heart is an ocean
I love without boundaries or restraint
It drowns people
My love is beautiful and scary
Perfect for strange creatures to live in
But attractive to everyone who loves
Sunsets, margaritas, a bit of splashing around
And getting their toes wet
I speak in waves to keep away weak swimmers
I thrash and lull and carry you so floaty
When you need me I have oxygen
When things aren't where I want them
Whole cities get swept away
And everything we've built will fall into me
Decayed, eroded, crumbled
I can take it all
There's graveyards of lovers on the floors of my soul
I spend days dreaming about rivers, divers and islands
I can cover in a kiss

All of my Snipple Snapples

Part 3:

1. Ghost Story

A million billion billion years ago someone put a ghost in a bottle and forgot about it sitting down there in the basement. The ghost was never dead. It was always alive. It sat there thinking, sleeping, and watching people come and go. Now, a million billion billion years is a long time to think about things. I reckon this ghost had thought everything that it could several million billion times over. It loved to dream. Dreams was all it had.

Sometimes the ghost wanted to rock its bottle off the bookshelf so it'd crash to the floor. Not necessarily to get away but just because it needed a sensation. It wanted to get thrown across the room, across the world, just not across forever. The ghost didn't want to rattle the place so the world would know he was there. Why should he? He just wanted someone to know already, to already know. He thought it was wrong to explain himself. He had a feeling in his ghost belly. He couldn't rock and couldn't crash or reach out. Mostly he just fell asleep.

After a while it didn't matter if he was awake or dreaming because he'd been in that bottle so long, all he could dream about was being in that bottle. He would dream that he was dreaming and couldn't see his dream ghost's dreams. So then he grew detached from himself and wondered what he was hiding. He split the bottle into two sides, one for dreaming and one for dreaming that you're dreaming. He kept himself to his own sides because he was no longer to be trusted.

Eventually he got sO SiCkK!!!of that GhOST! that he kicked him out and decided never to let him back in again. But while he was out there he didn't meet anyone he knew. You can only know someone so well and when you find someone you know as good as yourself you want to stay with them forever.

He missed himself & was lonely so he went back to the bottle to try and get back in. When he got there he found himself asleep. He knocked on the glass but the ghost wouldn't wake up. He waited for a long time just sitting there outside the bottle, wondering what he was dreaming about. He got so tired sitting there that he fell asleep against the glass.

It was about this time that the ghost inside woke up and saw him sleeping there. He wondered what he was dreaming about. Maybe what it's like to be in here cuz he's been in here so long dreaming about what it's like to be outside. That thought made him sick. He didn't ever wanna go out there. What good is it if you just go to sleep. He decided he'd just rather stay inside the bottle and dream about what the ghost was doing cuz to him, real life was a big disappointment.

2. Bottle Rockets in a Coffee Can

We were living in an immigrant apartment complex called The Capri, next door to a yet to be renowned child molester who would eventually be paroled to an address adjacent to an elementary school. The street we lived on used to be called Old Prison Road. Behind it was Buena Vista, which was about ten times worse than my street even though its name means, "good view." Good view of the crime scene maybe. There was a shooting every night. Which was out of place for the area. Only these two streets were bad.

The police were at our place constantly. I think instead of immigrants the complex was compounded by dick dads. I imagine the sane people would soon go crazy, having to call the cops so often. All of us getting beaten knew not to call when we heard screaming cuz that just meant getting hit harder when the police went away.

We got the place without ever having seen it. Some friends of our relatives, who didn't want us staying with them again and having things get crowded once we moved back from Oklahoma, put a word in for us. And since it was a shithole, we lived there for several years. I remember the journey well. We packed up like some real hillbillies on our way to open auditions for a modern day remake of The Grapes of Wrath

All of my Snipple Snapples

Once we got out of Texas, it started raining and things started coming apart. There were these Indians following us, picking up everything we dropped. They got our mattress. My bag of toys went flying and they pulled over to the side of the road to pick it up. I screamed, "Daddy, they got my toys!", He glanced down, sad & ashamed. "I know Leon." He gave me an "I'm sorry but there's nothing I can do about it" look, that showed he understood the pain and excitement a little boy has when he loses his toys to bandits.

He was afraid they were gunna scalp us! No matter what we dropped, he kept on trucking. While we're reliving the Joad's Odyssey through the dust bowl, I may as well get out of the way the few tidbits my eight year old mind retained of the trip. After the first time we ever ate at Sizzler, somewhere around Scottsdale, Arizona, we were looking to get back to the interstate when a lady crossing the street came a little too close to the car, meaning we had to slow down just a tiny bit. My dad had to growl at her because she wasn't family and didn't deserve to get pulled to the ground and have the living fuck beat out of her.

Another time a bee flew into my baby sister's nose and stung her. Except it wasn't a bee. My dad was driving a hundred miles an hour and the wind coming through the windows sent the cherry of his cigarette up my sister's nose. She would later pay for her nosiness by being thrown on the ground and having the living fuck beat out of her, once we got to our apartment, where she could be treated like family.

Once there, I soon became friends with this kid named Scott but not before he nearly ended my potential for romance with a tattoo bruising kick to my dick in a school yard fight, and I threw up on his shoes. His grandma was a drug dealer. She looked like a frog and smoked weed. Scott didn't have any parents. His dad was in jail for something. His mom just wasn't around.

I liked hanging out at Scott's house cuz he had lots of toys. We used to play legos and he'd make these sandwiches just like they sold at the gas stations, with the swiss cheese with the holes in it & the big pickle spears. I wasn't allowed to eat any of the food at my house but I could cook tea and sometimes, if no one was home I would have eggs. So I liked being at Scott's house better.

Sometimes he had stuff to do and he couldn't play. Then I'd just go somewhere else, like the mall even though it was far away and I'd get in trouble if my parents found out. The fun of reading comic books for hours and maybe buying an ice cream far outweighed my chance of getting busted. Which still wasn't as bad as getting caught at home, where my dad insisted on my chopping onions. He'd often lure me into hanging around the apartment with the promise of going for a dip in the complex pool. Even if I didn't want to swim he'd make me chop onions. I hate onions. To this day I hate onions. I don't mind chopping them anymore though. I lost my sense of smell to random violence & a broken nose from some hooligan I never saw at a punk concert. The leader of the band sat down and talked to me. It was cool. He was nice. Of course I was covered in blood and needed surgery. But onions never made me cry after that. I'm hitting back. Childhood damage crumbles like broken bones when you put a little "umph!", into it.

So me & Scott were best friends. This was quite a feat in itself because he was in Mr. Fleischman's class. Mr. Fleischman was a total prick. He told his whole class not to play with me. A bit outlandish, I know, but it's true. He said I was weird but I'm over all that now. What people don't know they can't use against you. Scott didn't care. After he kicked me in the dick we became close friends ...after I beat the shit out of him for it. But he was tough. I think our not wanting to get sent to the principal's office any more is what did it.

One time we decided we were gunna make a ton of dough. Old Prison Road was chock full of apartment buildings and each one had a dumpster. We figured all these immigrant asshole dick dads drank beer and that meant cans and cans mean money. Me & Scotty invested (and when I say invested, I only mean we took them from our kitchens) in some thick black plastic garbage bags. We jumped from dumpster to dumpster, getting our Pay-Less shoes all dirty and our thrift store clothes more thriftable, till we smelled like sweet piss & confectionaries. Come the end of the week, we filled our illegal

All of my Snipple Snapples

shopping cart three times. We threw our booty into the back of Scott's grandma's pinto and headed on down to the local recycling center.

Fifteen bucks! We split it Three dollars each and gave nine to grandma. She chipped in a buck and with that ten dollars sent her coke connection, an albino colored fella name of Snow, down to Mexico for some illegal(!)fireworks. The legal kind are more expensive cuz they don't come from Mexico and not as fun and not illegal so they're no good.

Grandma burst into our unruly game of legos and discarded sandwich crusts toking reefer and holding the kind of bag eight year olds would cream over, if they knew what creaming was. Cherry bombs, fire crackers and bottle rockets, hundreds of bottle rockets. Our summer was set.

Snow showed us this trick where you drill a hole in the top of a coffee can, put a fire cracker in it and set the can on a plate of water. When the fire cracker goes off -BLAMMO!- it sends the can 30 feet in the air. I don't know why children love explosions any more than I know why people take up smoking. It's just one of those things people think are cool that gets them into trouble.

One day we were setting off bottle rockets in the coffee can. We had been all over lighting them, holding them in our hands. But I really wanted a sandwich. So we headed back on our skateboards and played Coleco for a while. Then we both had sandwiches and a Pepsi (another contraband item left off my family shopping list) and decided to shoot rockets off Scott's front porch. His house was right on a major intersection and tons of people saw us. But it was two days till the Fourth of July and we were just some kids who got itchy.

On our twelfth go, a rocket fizzled onto a neighbor's roof and exploded with the force of some Tijuana packing routine gone wrong. It blew up and we ran. We were young and scared and we both ran home. Except Scott's home was a lot closer to the burning building than mine. So when the police burst in through his door and pulled him out from underneath his bed crying like a baby who knew they were gunna get their ass whipped, they never would have believed a boy from Mr. Fleischman's class would have been burning houses down with me. Not when I lived so far down the block. Besides he never said anything. He was too scared to speak, and by the time he realized he could have dobbed me in for half the blame, it was too late. He had been sent up north to live with his uncle on a cattle farm past Modesto. While I counted the boys and girls coming out of the apartment next door carrying candy bars and the days till my dad left when we finally got out of that hell hole.

3. James Dean

It was a welfare motel afternoon when the sun hung us out to dry like hot peppers on beds of pins and needles. The denizens of room 302 had cotton fever. While the younger children had cotton mouths with hungry land bellies they've been killing off by the way of brain cells, it's that wacky tobaccy. They just can't figure out how to get from hand to mouth. With the parents ignoring them, exhausted in their laziness, incapable of adulthood, tiny children and their families watch cartoons and feed each other drugs because they can't afford food. On the great pinnacle of television that is a slap in the face, children aged zero to never mattered are interrupted to bring them a special bulletin. "Please kill yourself. We will put you on tv." The family watches and learns as the angry middle aged H.I.V positive white male takes his health maintenance organization complaint to live broadcast off the harbor freeway and writes it out to cameras with a shotgun blast using his brain.

Nobody cares and the children aren't surprised because they know this already. They've learned it from A.D.D., fetal alcohol syndrome, starvation, malnutrition and the ugly pain of Christmas morning. So when the little kid in room 302 stutters trying to tell me something, I listen hoping it won't be what he's told me every day for the past six months. "H-H-H-Hey, Hey Leon did you see that guy...he blew hith fyuggn brainth out." I want to tell him to forget it but he can't. That image is inside his head huffing and puffing at how fucked up things are. I figure someday it'll hit home and he'll blow the house down.

4. 9:22 on a Tuesday Night

The blue, the blue is cornhusk crayon colored with white waxy starry flecks a million miles away dying. I'm driving with my neck crookd. This is why I should get a convertible. The sky's a whole different world up there. I work in the sewer and try to stare through the holes in manhole covers towards heaven, the second heaven. With all the gasses down here you have to watch your cigarette or things could get hellish real quick. Then you'd die and go to the second hell. I guess I've discovered purgatory. I should invite some Catholics.

On my way to work, I always go past that empty lot when I turn on Washington. It reminds of a mansion that Errol Flynn built in a movie but was torn down . I want to sit there sometimes and get spiritual. I'd probly fall asleep. All that relaxing makes me woozy.

My car's blue you know, an old 78 Ford Fairmont that I drive 100 miles an hour on a slow day up the freeway just waiting for someday the mountain mud'll catch me cuz the law often does. I really should slow down. Once I had a dream about these 50 foot spiders in Brazil with machetes that patrolled the fields like police and in that dream I was driving 180 on an empty freeway, lapping up air and sunshine like a stupid dog at the apex of life but then these vines that had been growing on patchwork grids across the city sprung up and started chasing me. They were the size of skyscrapers and they tossed me up like a chicken nugget to their maw. Then I went to Antarctica and battled the devil who was a snowman. The sky looked like that in my dream, the way it does now, corn husk blue with waxy white crayon colored spotted stars that never died cuz I made up that I remembered them and planted them in a manmade electromagnetic universe like a virus to eat up braincells and dream drive in a million other peoples' snowy nightmares. I'm a bit ambitious.

But instead I go to work. It has steps this empty lot. Which is one reason it makes me think of a crumbled old mansion, brick steps like someone took a lot of care tending to a dead world. I could get so spiritual there, me and all those ghosts going sleepy for dreaming up devils in any manner we choose with crayons and snowballs where I could reach into the sky and get enough stars to make my very own adversary/dragos/devil/don't believe oh yule have a warm reception. I feel sorry for the people who don't believe in hell or believe in the devil but not god. They're kind of stupid really and it's rather like believing in death without believing people ever live.

I park my car about a meter from the cafeteria where the large yellow windows look moons and I can see the moon from them and if I walk halfway up the steps to the cafeteria and stand on my toes, I can see the whole night skyline of Los Angeles which isn't really that impressive but is pleasant none the less.

Me and Jimmy will be working together tonight on section g, installing a transformer box for the third grid out east a bit, near Alhambra. Seems the world is growing and there's not enough electricity for everyone's vacuum cleaners, sonic tooth brushes and rechargeable dildos. Jimmy's a little younger than me but I'm not that old. I feel I'll be telling myself that more and more as time progresses towards what?, its end I presume, like a star that goes to hell cuz it has no heaven to believe in cuz it's in the sky and thinks that's all there is. But I'm down here. Maybe there'll be some other time. All god has to do is flip the little egg timer hour glass and spit a new kind of shit. I heard he's got styles.

Me and Jimmy head down the tunnel from the hallway about 30 feet and a left turn pass the locker room. I have to put on my work boots, rubber soles, rubber toes, flanks, all that jazz. I go through about 6 pairs a year and its tough getting the nurse to give me another pair when we're only allotted one a year but I tell her I work in the sewer and there's alligators down there and all sorts of shit. I could get hepatitis. You work up here with lights and sunshine. There's no alligators. It's rough work getting those rubber boots. Jimmy brings extra gloves and a pack of gum. He's been trying to quit smoking but who wants to put things in their mouth when you lean on your knuckles for a second and your hands get dipped in shit. I bring a book I've been reading on the possible ancient correlations between Gaelic & Arab mythology. Apparently, it's based on a shamrock fossil they found in the desert in a lil oasis 40 miles north of Dubai and local legends of a black leprechaun painted on a wall in a small seaside village in County Cork that no one can remember the exact location of, wink wink. It's pretty interesting.

All of my Snipple Snapples

Me and Jimmy stop for a break. He gets out a ham sandwich he got at a local gas station, wrapped in what looks like twice used saran and starts to tell me about his brother's girlfriend and the way they fuck like people on tv which is how Jimmy wants to fuck but he don't know no girls with pay per view that you don't pay for cuz no one pays for pay per view but his brother has it on one of those black box descramblers and that's where they learned to fuck. I try to ignore him and turn on my flashlight, one of those head jobs fastened to my helmet with a rubber band and a cheap battery. Our break is as long as we care to inhale what you flush down your toilets or out the window, cuz remember, storm drains lead to the ocean and trash can choke the dolphin turtle puppies but I don't mind it cuz it gives me something to step on and chokes the alligators too. I'm almost to the end of my book when my little light goes out and Jimmy says not to worry he's got a light. I should point out, Jimmy is a rebel. He crossed his arms in kindergarten and decided not to learn about reading cuz when was recess? and he wasn't gunna take this shit so Jimmy doesn't wear a helmet. I'm hoping I'll make it to the end before it's time to get back to work and fold my page over in the corner to mark my place. Jimmy pulls out his light and smokes up, lighting the emergency cigarette he has to have cuz this sandwich tastes like shit and I'm dying for a smoke, c'mon.

Unfortunately, dangerous gas looms ever present but Jimmy doesn't know that. Give the guy a break. He can't read the signs. He's going back to school for that though cuz he can't figure out how to work the pay per view and damn he's horny. He needs to find a hefty Latin broad to move in with him who's really got an itch to scratch and wash dishes. So mix sewers, cigarettes lighters and life what you get? A big boom. Those evolutionists are right. Is that the end? I don't know. I'm charcoal in a big white star booming through the underground while all those dildos and sonic toothbrushes go uncharged. I gave my life for em you know. I must be some kind of Jesus. This must be some kind of heaven.

5. Arroyo Secco

Usually raindrops run down the window and clean the earth but in this story there are no raindrops. The earth is hot & dusty, scorched. The cactuses dig deep & can stand still for years, saving water to keep on living. If you had any water and you wanted to build a house you would scrape up the mud and do it brick by brick. But the mud is hard. It takes hammers and tools, sharp points. Hidalgo has some. His father left them. They're wrapped in a brown cloth his father had since the days of the factory, when he put cars together & stamped Ford, American Made, cheaply down in Mexico.

Father died in his rocking chair from a tooth infection. He believed in modern medicine, prayed fervently and would never see a doctor, on account of him dying having never seen a doctor. What did they look like ...men in white coats? How come they didn't get dirty, all this dust blowing? The ants must think it's gunna rain. They'll die focused on the sun as Hidalgo stoops to see them in his glasses. God came down and he hated us. He had eyes of fire and killed everyone. I'm the only one that got away. We must be strong.

His mother brought them back for him one day from Mexico City. She had to ride two days. No one knows why she went. Hidalgo never needed glasses but now he had to have them to see. His vision had declined to meet the exact prescription. They were just a present. She hoped her son would grow up to be a doctor. All the doctors wore them.

She's gone now. One day when she was crossing the street a truck hit her & she disappeared. Gone like the vapor. His brothers & sisters ran away into the desert chasing rattlesnakes & coyotes, playing in dingy yellow t-shirts with Hawaii slogans silk screened on the front that drifted here from Korea. They ran like nymphs into the mountains, growing blacker & blacker. One day they'll return, sun bleached Arabs, big chested, telling Hidalgo about their kingdom in the sun with beautiful mermaids, ten foot tuna, great big swordfish and friendly bears that share their honey.

He has to build a house for them. So when they return they'll be able to find him and have somewhere to spend the night.

The old house, uncle fell asleep smoking. God receive his soul. Hell screamed for Hidalgo and he saw an awful demon reaching his claws out. Pull me from the window. But Hidalgo couldn't be responsible for unleashing Hell unto the world. Eventually it went away. Very few things were left, amongst them were his father's tools.

You have to kill the cactus to keep on living. You have to chop off its arms, its surrendering arms that have no weapons. Friend, see, I have nothing. Please. You have to try to make the ground wet and hope you have enough tears to build a new house.

6. Pueblo Bonito

From his ranch, Pedro could see the ocean. It was a small ranch, hardly a farm, a garden really. Actually it was only a tree and two dogs and Pedro didn't own the land either. He was only a squatter. But if a man works the land it belongs to him.

Well it was hard work peeling manzanas but the dogs had to eat. Pedro loved those animals. That's why he sacrificed so much. The vitamins are in the peel, you know. If he didn't care he would've eaten the whole apple himself and let the dogs wander the beach hunting for fish.

Pedro couldn't stand fish. He couldn't stand the thought of his mutts having to eat fish. So he kept them close by & fed them apple peels. Fish tasted like Pedro's mother. Pedro hated eating his mother. He vowed on his life to never do it again. And since she was already gone, he didn't have to worry about that happening.

They were going to start anew. Four families including Pedro's own had to pass through the mountains on the way to the promised land. Pedro's father had some friends on a fishing boat. There was this seaside village where you could live easy, drink tequila, stare at the ocean and bask in the sun like a turtle.

But misfortune overtook them. One of the mules ran away. Marcitos took off to find him, and the families couldn't leave without

Marcitos. He was such a handsome boy. Everybody loved him. By the time it had sunk in that Marcitos wasn't coming back the wind had started, then the snow. Which they would've beaten because they had left a few days ahead of schedule to allow for such disaster, but the loss of Marcitos, who was the navigator, and the mule, who had the maps & food, left the families stuck in the snow starving.

Little Connie passed away because Marcitos wasn't there to remind her to take her medicine. The families were so hungry, even though it went against God, they ate her. Surely, God would understand. Otherwise he wouldn't have made her taste so good. At the end of it all, the only two left were Pedro & his mother. Luckily, she was a fat woman and got him through the winter. It had to be done. She had thought about eating Pedro but he was only skin & bones. There was no meat on him.

Now, he was here, sleeping next to his dogs, browning in the sunshine and staring out to sea. There were manzana trees closer to the beach but Pedro couldn't see the turtles from down there. Pedro loved the turtles. He'd never seen anything like em, humongous giant things with flippers & shells all the colors of the rainbow. They lived on an island two spits past the shore. From his ranch up on the hill, beneath his tree, Pedro could watch them all he pleased.

To each turtle he gave a name; Cabron, Esmeralda, Pitito, Salvador, Juarez, Leon y Chuy. Occasionally he'd forget which one was which. You'd think this wouldn't matter but to cover his forgetfulness Pedro supposed the turtle whose name he'd forgotten was a relative visiting from out of state; Tio Carlos, Tia Chele or Chato, the cousin with a few screws loose.

So Pedro did nothing but sleep, eat apples & watch turtles. His dogs did the same. Pedro probably would have spent his whole life this way. He practically had. It'd been 51 years since Pedro first moved under the apple tree but there were hotels coming. Mexico was a popular resort destination. People needed to get away back to simpler times, such lovely weather.

All of my Snipple Snapples

    Pedro's hilltop was a local point of interest. From there you could see the only surviving group of Large Parrot Shell Turtles known to man; an ecological gem in their natural habitat. The hotel was to be called Emerald Cove, on account of the green water and that most turtles are green. So when people think of turtles, they think Emerald Cove.

    A few men showed up with a bit of money. Pedro didn't own the land but technically since he'd been occupying it for so long he did have a legal right to its ownership under Mexican law. So the resort couldn't just kick him off. Fifty one years is a long time. Besides, the resort wanted to avoid trouble. Paying him off was the easiest way. When they showed him the money, Pedro mumbled something through his few cracked teeth & started spitting apple seeds at them.

    The men left the money there, American dollars. He could use it to buy some clothes, get rid of that wacky fur coat. It looks like dog hair. He could move into a nice apartment, drink martinis, get some fancy sunglasses and some skin lotion. Maybe meet a woman before he dies. But Pedro planned on living another thirty years. This money wouldn't last that long and where would he find another ranch like this. There were no other turtles with such pretty colors on their backs. He had no more relatives to eat, no dogs either. All he had was here in front of his eyes and beneath this apple tree.

    Maybe he could move in with the turtles disguised as an out of state relative. He took the American money and bought a fancy colored jacket. Since he had nothing to pack, he just up & left. That was his move. He would be Chato's cousin, Guerro, on account of how dark he'd gotten baking in the sun all these years. He swam the three minutes out to sea and explained to the turtles that he was just visiting. Could they spare some room?

    The turtles were unreceptive. They'd been watching the man for quite some time now and weren't impressed by his cheap disguise or broken Spanish. In Ecuador, the Spanish was much finer. Ahhhh, Ecuador. Those were swingin' times. One of the turtles, I believe it was Chuy, pointed out perhaps his poor Spanish had less to do with his nationality & more to do with his ugly teeth. Juarez & Salvador agreed.

Though the turtles ignored him, Pedro enjoyed life on the rock. The turtles grew to not be so disgusted by him as much and occasionally they all enjoyed a swim together & a sunning on the beach. There was one problem though, Pedro was growing increasingly more hungry.

From time to time a boat full of gringos would motor up to the rock and tell Pedro through their loudspeaker, he had to leave. Go to Miami. Go to L.A. Try Puerto Vallarta. People would be coming to see giant turtles, not some old man. What happened to all the money they gave him? They weren't going to give him any more. He hadn't lived on this island long enough.

One day, a great storm came and though it hadn't snowed in the village for over a hundred years before the turtles came, it began to snow. Everyone was in a panic. The turtles didn't know what to do. They huddled close together and rubbed shells. Since it was snowing, all the fish had froze and the turtles were beginning to starve. The first turtle to go was Cabron. He was the oldest. Though it made them sad, they all had a piece of Cabron, all except Pedro. He thought turtles might taste like fish since they lived in the ocean. So, he wouldn't have any part of it. As each turtle froze, the other turtles grew fat & warm, till all that was left was the skinny old man & Cousin Chato ...I think. Finally Chato couldn't escape the cold and as his time came. He begged Pedro, don't be foolish. He was one of them. He had to go on living. Eat me and survive. Well, Pedro gave in. He couldn't take the hunger anymore.

When the sun came back out all that was left on the island were turtle shells and a slightly chubby old man. Now what were the hoteliers to do? You can't have a turtle resort without giant rainbow shelled turtles of the sea. Then Mayno over in Ideas had a great idea. Why not just get new turtles and paint them. No one would know the difference except the old man and no one could understand him anyway.

All of my Snipple Snapples

So, Mayno got a bunch of turtles and spray painted them in his garage. Everything would be okay. The resort would go ahead as planned and Pedro would make new friends. But Pedro had never had nothing to look at before. He sat there and sat there till he couldn't take it anymore and he died of boredom. As Pedro's body was washing out to sea, Mayno came and unloaded all the new turtles. They loved it on their new home. People came from all over the world to see them and the big hotel made lots of money.

7. A Piggy Tale

Every time I'm here I think of that Prince song, well... except sometimes I think of nothing at all. I just do my job. You get used to it, trained. Human beings can get used to anything. It's how we adapt. All that Darwin stuff.

They give me a taser, the big kind. It's sad. It really is. The worst thing, well besides death, is the painting. The mural covering the whole outside. It's infamous. The only painting in this town. The only thing for people to look at. Pigs runnin', pigs playin', picnic pigs rollin' in the mud. It's horrible. They bring them here on this evil trip. The roots of duplicity go back to their childhood homes. They get packed onto these trucks with holes like little windows. First time they ever see the city. Pigs are smart. They were probly looking forward to visiting a museum. They truck 'em on down from Fresno right through DTLA.

They stick their little piggy snouts out the window, wondering what a skyscraper is. Probly thinking about lunch. Then here it is. This great mural. Oh, happy day. An amusement park, some cultural enrichment. We're gunna play inside. Wilbur was so happy to sit next to his best friend. They're marched off the bus single file. All the good children stay in line, except they're excited you know. They snort & snistle, trying not to pee but it's a long trip. It's hard keeping it in.

Now, I don't know what it sounds like when the doves cry. I can't imagine many people want to eat any of those. Maybe where Prince is from, they like 'em covered in ice cream. But around here we stick to hog. They lock the gates, shave 'em. I've even heard some of the old timers down from the farms in Mexico like to have their way with them. Which is a ruined field trip enough, getting raped in a warehouse, living through all of the flesh slapping stinging your ears, hearing a belt buckle jingle and click, watching them pulling their pants up and thinking that the worst is over, wiping the snot from your nose and trotting off rubbing your flanks back to your friends, hoping all the mascara hasn't poured off your eyes but knowing you're a mess.

Then they bring 'em to me. I have to look at the first one sitting their nice and pretty, unscathed. Long eye lashes smiling. Hello. Old spotlights hang from I-beams beneath the tin roof. One lights up Marnie & I beside ten of her friends. They sway a little and I tell her, now Marnie, this ain't got nothing to do with you, but before that I pat her on the head, rubbing her ears like a kitten. I want her to know she's a good girl but before I finish my sentence, the taser's at her throat, cooking. You can smell her tail uncurl.

All the other pigs start screaming. Screaming!

They scream like you or me. Like there's a murderer pulling back the shower curtain. They cry and they shit themselves. Their vocal cords tear but they don't stop. I kill every one of them. The sounds of struggle, the rustle of escape, it dies against chains and straps till all that's left is a smell, till the last pig takes his wings and Bob comes in with a hose to clean the shit up.

8. Random Drunk

Jim Beam, Jim beam did something no one, not even the ancient Greeks could ever figure out. He turned fire into water, kept it burning and churned that shit out till the whole world was blazing.

"Gimme one more. I gotta go to work."

Sam signals. Sam plays the pokies. Sam hangs out in the pub all day and leaves his dog waiting at the door. Plenty of people in the neighborhood know the dog but'd never seen Sam.

All of my Snipple Snapples

Sam downs a hefty glass and adjusts his testicles. His keys jingle as he pulls his pants up. They've been sliding off for about thirty years now.

"See you later."

Sam steps out of the cave covered stale asshole of a room onto the sidewalk. His dog sits up and Sam scruffs its head. Sam looks around like something's changed. Same black grey pavement, cracks in the sidewalk, downward sloping street and poplar trees. Same breeze, bicycle messengers and small boring sedans. Same birds & children playing off in the distance. A radio somewhere, same hum in your ears, same sound of the world turning.

Sam pulls up his zipper. The dog sees Sam has something important to say, something menacing. Sam has taken an important pause to signify this.

"……..gotta go to work."

The dog nods. The dog's known it's been time to go to work for quite a while now. He knows because the pretty lady in the Iron Maiden shirt stopped by and patted his head twenty minutes ago. The dog likes the way she smells. He always smiles at her and licks his teeth. She never gets the hint. Once in a while she rubs his belly.

Sam hops in his tow truck. His dog is already there. The dog has its own set of keys. Once Sam lost his and came up with a brilliant idea, make copies for the dog. But since Sam'd always forget him there on the curb and just drive off thus voiding the whole point of Dog even having his own keys, the dog started letting himself into the truck. He didn't like waiting around anymore than he had to. Dog liked rides. He liked pretending he was a movie star and sticking his head out the window. Sometimes people waved. The dog wondered why he wasn't a person. They always had shit to eat. Just once he'd like to go into a store and eat whatever he wanted. It was a pipe dream doggy. Society kept him down.

Sam turned on the radio. Skynard. Skynard rocked. Sam liked to sing along.

'Baby be a simple… sing it ya fucker."

He scratched his dog vigorously. They were best friends.

"Whew!"

That's the onomonpeic sound of blue & red lights turning, cop cars pulling up beside you and pointing out you stupid fucker, you're going the wrong way.

"Pull over."

He has a booming voice. Probly works in radio

This is a scary time for Sam. Sam's been arrested twice for DUI. A third and they take his license, take his truck, maybe even take his dog. It's animal endangerment ya know. No truck means no job. No job means no money, no house, no liquor. He'd fucking starve.

Sam guns it. He hits 80 from zero in ten and the chase is on.

Sam knows these streets. Sam lives these streets. Over there he lost his virginity at the age of five. Down the street was his first kiss, age 15. A couple blocks up, he used to play stick ball. He drives past a blue building and remembers Megan. God they were in love.

Sam turns left and the cops are right behind him. Skynard's still ringing in his ears. They're flooded with adrenalin. He ain't even drunk no more. Dog sticks his head out the window. This shit's too windy. He decides to go to sleep. Now this'd be a job, bein' a race car driver. Peeling down city streets. Sam sees it now. A life big as the smile cross his face. The cops bump him.

"Wo ho!" He laughs.

"Pull over!"

All of my Snipple Snapples

Sam's sure he knows that voice. I think he announces at the races. It's all brick buildings and warehouses now. Sam knows he's got 'em. Just over the tracks there. But that's what they're probly expecting. Cops are trained for this sort of shit. They know the criminal mind. Ol' Sam he decides to out think 'em. He spins the wheel around to head the other way but his big old truck ain't no Countach. It rolls at 80 mph across the intersection then skids crashing into a bus stop knocking down an electrical poll and killing 11 people. They never saw him coming. He pinned the whole lot against the wall and squished 'em like jelly sandwiches, 'cept for the one dragged beneath his passenger door. He got scraped to pieces, just a smear. They were reading papers, wearing headphones, just tired on their way home from work, poor people leaving children behind. Calls'll have to be made overseas to the Ukraine, Cambodia, Mexico. Someone will have to email Zaire and visit the western suburbs.

For six blocks the city goes dark. Factories shut down. Millions of dollars in potential revenue are cut with wasted man hours and computer repair. Product will have to be scrapped.

Sam's legs are pinned behind his head and his dog is in the glove compartment. Sam doesn't hurt though. He's part spider. The cop steps up and laughs.

"Sir, I'm gunna need you to get out of the vehicle."

He says it every time. It always cracks him up. He's saving this one for the tonight show. He's finally got a decent gig. A one liner. Ah, I know it's small but everyone has to start somewhere.

9. letters from ninimosa
long days we sailed through precious darkness
in search of promised dreams
the ss sealy was a strong and sturdy ship
i was the captain and twee my first mate
our expedition led us to a distant archipelago
far removed from any main land

miles from shore
we found our ship to be stuck in the bog
and disembarked
carrying pillows through the everglades
something to trade with the natives
twee kept our spirits chirp with little songs
hand crafted, right there on the spot
one i believe was about a pony
named tony
after three days of trudging through this slop
i saw a bear peeking at us from behind a tree
immediately i alerted twee
mid crescendo in an ode to breakfast cereal
he was really caught up in
he looked but saw no bear
and sang me a liar
oh yure a liar captain, he sang
a dirty liar doodoodoo
as he stroked an imaginary violin
maybe i was
the bear turned the corner quickly
before i could get a photograph
and we moved on
perhaps the dreams these islands offered were crap
but readily available
quick delusions like pop-tarts sprung from a vending machine
that don't really satisfy yure daily nutritious requirements
but keep you going
so on we went.....

10. Trailer Talking
"Aintchyu kitty, aintchyou?"

My little black and white hillbilly girl. She arches her back and raises her tail and rubs her head against the fist-&-knuckle of my index finger like I was the best lover in the world.

She's so tiny. She weighs about a pound, pound and a half. I just pick her up in my hand like a big glass of Pepsi.

All of my Snipple Snapples

"Daddy loves you. Come here. Kiss me. That's right."

This little kitty is my BEST friend. I look into her eyes and I kiss her, and I hold her under my neck. I hold her tight. She's so good. Well hell, she's got lights in her eyes like the stars up in the Hollywood Hills, my little kitten does. I'm gunna name her Sarah.

See, I just found her. It was raining & I heard a little meow at my trailer door so I went and checked on it, and there was this little kitty sitting all proper like, introducing herself. So I got her a bowl of milk & we just set down.

It's been raining pretty hard. All the electricity went so I just got a flashlight next to my lamp, and me & Sarah are sitting by the tv.

"I got some tuna."

So she follows me. Dancing, running fast, pawing up my leg like it'll make the can opener go any faster.

"Here you go Sarah. Eat it up."

I reckon she came out them woods there. There's lots of cats. Lots of trees to climb and piss on. She looks like Ava Gardener.

I went in those woods once, well I go in every now & then, but just this particular time of the instance I'm telling, I found a playground, a playground in the middle of the woods. Now when I was young, the trees was our playground. We used to run around spitting like some feisty cats, swingin' from the branches.

There was a slide, some swings, a little jungle gym. I did some checking around, asked Billy at the grocery store. Turns out the people who lived here before me had some children that was allergic to the sunshine. So they had to go out & play at night.

One day they played so hard they fell asleep. When the sun came up they done turned into a pile of ashes. Parents got sad & just moved away. That's how I got the place so cheap. But nobody told me till I asked.

Sarah seen it all, didn't you little kitty? You reckon cats tell tales? Meow meow meow meow, and just sit around the campfire roasting little mices on sticks like they were marshmallows. Micemallows.

"Don't go past there kits. You see that slide. That's where the children died and if you walk by they'll gettyA!!"

He would point with his paw (the older kitty telling the story), the younger kittins would shiver & huddle together spookidly.

I'm a little afraid to go past there myself. I reckon it's haunted. It's just a quiet place y'know, one you walk past & can tell something strange is there cuz you're looking at nothing but you feel like it's looking back at you. I figure them children might be mad at me for moving into their house and've gone crazy cuz their parents left 'em.

Maybe they play all night long cuz they're sad and they're trying to forget that they're not alive anymore. Maybe if I go out there they might talk to me but maybe they might hang me up around my neck & throat with the swing chain. N' while I'm dying, all the cats in the forest will run to see me turn purple. They'll sit there attentively staring at my dead body. Then one of them children ghost'll say, "boo!", and all the cats will get scared & move into my trailer cuz they're afraid of the woods. They'll be cats sleeping in my bed and watching tv, drinking liquor.

You would try and keep it down Sarah, but there'd be too many of 'em. One day you'd come home from work in your little business suit & theyd've set the place on fire with their card games and sandwiches. They'd just plum forget they left the iron on.

I think we'd just better stay in here. What'd you think?

Quiet huh? At least you could meow to amuse me. Come over here. Sit here. You play card games? I'ma show you how to play pinochle. It's windy. I think we just better stay inside.

11. Sweet Tooth

When I was a child my parents put me on a plane back to Los Angeles where I spent my days hanging out with my uncle at the snack bar in South Gate Park, eating all the candy I could dream of. This caused tooth problems, which led to extensive dental work as a small child which led to a lot of blood which was traumatizing. The dentist was my biggest fear and for years I didn't go. Somewhere in my mid 20s, I had to get my wisdom teeth pulled and I went to the doctor that my mom had been cashing out my unused dental insurance with to buy us Christmas presents. Years later she was my cousin's drug dealer and cousins on both sides of the family have punched her in the face on separate occasions, while she was working on them. She also gave my ex-wife a root canal, finished and announced, "Aw man. That's the wrong tooth." Additionally, she once dropped a needle down my throat and screamed, "Don't move!" So... she caused some problems. Her work was bad, eventually I lost teeth. Now, I'm lying in bed, jaw aching as it does these days, misaligned, teeth throbbing because somewhere under cheap caps, a nerve is aching. But who knew, ya know, that a child eating a candy bar and an adult reeling in pain could be so connected across time. It's like a rainbow bridge of mistakes.

12. No Fan

There's nothing like a garage shack 2:30 in the afternoon both windows closed, curtains shut just baking sweat cake inside while the family's gone. You got that dirty little girl from down the street on your brother's bed, only socks and rosary beads, roaches singing hallelujahs in the kitchen to the slap slap slap. Ain't nothing like it.

Prayers still linger in the corner from your mother's knees, 6am. Thank you for the sunshine. The smell of grease and sex is too much for one tiny house to hold. It sweats through cracks in the building and the neighbors wonder what's cooking.

If you could grab a thought from this little girl's mind it might slow that pound pound heart of yours down to a tingle. Her fingers swoop across the carpet like a musketeer from a chandelier before she grabs back on, grabs your behind hnnnnns and smiles. Brown old pile

Leon McConnell

that it is, she thinks of her teddy bear, mom out the door and the moon barely lighting her bed sheets.

Grandma'd curl next to her, stay all night long, shhh don't be afraid of the dark. Except she wasn't afraid of the dark, she was afraid of the prayers her grandma made her say in the dark. "If I die before I wake…" So she had sex with the lights on remembering teddy's evil grin while grandma snored.

You smile. She forgets what she's thinking about. Your sweat drips down her nose and rolls till it's lost, somewhere in her neck, somewhere in the bed. It feels funny. Sorry. She tries to take her socks off no hands but her toes are stuck inside, impeded and don't work.

The door slams. Hearts explode. O my God! O my God! You say it too. Oh my God …and you're both underneath the bed huffing be quiet; sweat pouring down your face, you dripping down her leg. Your prayers stuck under the bed where God can't reach them run to the corner, mix with your mother's and try to make a happy family.

Sweat, cum and girl umm soak into the floor pool and cool down. Is it hotter than hell in here? No wonder this place smells. Roaches run from an old bag of Cheetos long forgotten, giggling thanks for lunch and it's alarming. You bump oww! your head, shit! Sorry. But she's sleeping. She's holding on tight and sleeping. Her skin feels nice. She's pretty here under the bed too and gets you hard again. Then you think she's even kinda nice with her clothes on. Then you think about marrying her. Door slams!

Hey, get up! High heels click down the sidewalk, click click back to the liquor store with a five dollar bill. Hmm. Her eyes rub. You hungry? Hhmmm. Smile. You smile too. That's nice. It's the first time you ever wanted to make anyone lunch.

Don't forget to thank God who took your prayers, saved your ass …and the prayers of your mother who prayed her son wouldn't be so lazy all the time. And thank God who answered the prayers of that dirty little girl from down the street who held tight onto your ass and her rosary beads almost the entire time, clutching, keeping you close. God, give me a baby. God, thank you. Hallelujah.

13. Night Shift

Andre & Judie lived in Tulsa. Judie worked in a factory making milky plastic baby bottles for fake children. Andre worked midnight to six at the gas station. Mostly that involved sitting in the parking lot smoking cheap cigarettes too close to the gasoline. He had long black hair that hung over his face like seaweed on underwater monsters as they take their first steps onto shore. Judie wore hers short like David Bowie on the cover of his Hunky Dory album. She had freckles. Andre had earrings and a penchant for black metal band t-shirts. They were in love as any two anythings that had ever walked the earth. So I guess you could say they were the most in love people ever that anyone ever knew.

Andre liked to kiss Judie in places she said she didn't like to be kissed. Her knees, elbows, wrists, the small of her back, down her fingers, up her legs, on her belly, her neck, her ears, her nose, her lips, eyes, and everywhere in between. He thought she was lying and built his love for kissing her on this disbelief. Judie wondered why she said she didn't like kisses when they felt so good and was sure she didn't like them regardless.

Please stop... you keep getting me all sticky. Andre stopped with three tiny little kisses in a triangle on her neck, moved over and adjusted his erection. Judie got up and straightened her shirt.

Do you want some dinner?
I'll eat at work?
Nachos?
I like nachos.
Yeah, but they're not good for you.
They got cheese and I put some jalapenos on em.
That's vegetables, protein and vitamin c. It's practically nutritious.

She hmmd, turned her head and went into the kitchen. Andre's erection subsided and as he got up to follow cutie pie, he found it didn't give him too much trouble. He pulled his hair back behind his ears. She always thought he looked cute this way and wondered what he'd look like with short hair like a normal boy. Then she wondered what she'd look like with long hair. It's been so long she can't remember. She thought he looked so damn hmmmm. He had full pink lips the color of rose wine and always looked so concerned even when he got mad at the tv or the video games or the people who act like assholes when it's so easy to be nice.

Do you want some coffee?
I'm okay baby. Don't you... isn't like your favorite show gunna be on?
Yeah, are you sure? Why don't you have some coffee.

She started the kettle boiling and he smiled thank you and she smiled because she could do something to make him happy. She made it extra sweet, warm and as little like coffee as she was capable of doing while still ensuring the caffeine content would keep him awake.

The nights were boring at the gas station. Only the weirdoes fixed hat. Once Andre helped a guy clean his car with some windex and an old pair of white undies, the whole car. Then the guy bought him some nachos, offered him some clothes and said they had a room at his house. His wife wouldn't mind. I don't think he understood that Andre worked there, and that everyone out at 3:13 am wasn't homeless. Some of em just had jobs.

Oh, shit I got to go to work.

He grabbed his skateboard and jacket and rushed to the door, pushing a wet kiss onto Judie's cheek as he flew.

Hey, you forgot something.

He looked for his wallet, his keys. Where was the dog?

You forgot your four.
Oh.

He blushed and sat down.
Have fun…..soft lips say a lot…kiss
Do a good job…it's like a dance, back again….kiss
Be careful, be safe and alert. I need you to come home safe to me
   …again
I love you…..kiss, hold, hmmmm kiss
I love you too (and when you say this it has to be as quiet as
possible in complete sincerity like nothing else could be truer)
   kiss
May this four hold you to the next…kiss
Kiss kiss
Kiss
Kiss kiss.

God knows why they called it a four, maybe because the thing lasted nearly four hours.

Shit, I'm gunna be late.
I love you
Good night.

The door closes. She lights up her cigarette, old punk rock posters cover the walls, the dingy walls. The tv comes on and it's a light show in primary colors. She sinks into the ten dollar sofa and exhales.

Uhhhhhhhhh.

The night is black. The night is good. Andre can't think of anywhere he'd rather live than Tulsa. It has trees. You can see the stars. This is good. Everything is good. It doesn't get any better than this.

14. Ivy & Decay
Angela had kisses like tendrils that crawled down from the moon on a spider string into the New Orleans night. They Ginger Rogers'd on me for just a hovering second. She tasted like morning glories. She was growing on me and her lips were flushed, probly from too much

biting. They were ready to make a red sea if she spoke any higher than a whisper or kissed any harder than a hush. I asked her why she bit them.

"How could I resist. They're really good you know."

I did. Angela was fourteen and liked to play with guns. We'd been living together off and on the bump of chance meetings round 3 or 4 am when either of us'd be going for a walk. The first time she took me to her castle by the bayou and showed me her collection.

"When my daddy died, I got the guns. When my mommy died, I got the house. When my uncle died, I got the place to myself and when I sicced the dogs on the child services people I finally got some peace and quiet around here. But it gets lonely."

I imagine it would. Nothing to do but put on flowing black dresses and wander the halls. She suggested we take some guns off the wall and play hide and seek. I was sneaking out of the pantry stealing a good chunk of cheese when she got me, straight in the heart.

"Bang! you're dead."

She smiled, sweeping her hair back, dropping her gun and coming to tend to my body. I loved her like some people love Disneyland. Yeah it's nice and you have a good time but it comes at a high price and the rats are huge. So we saw each other every now and again. Right now was one of those gains.

"How come I only see you at night Ang?"
"How come I only see YOU at night Dave? Are you a ghost?"
"Un uhh, a vampire."
"Oh, reeeally?"

She descended on me, tickling ooga booga, climbing into my lap, fingers surf temples to the neck. She pulls me in with both hands and kicks me in the eye lashes with tiny little legs line dancing, Rockettes, and kisses too hard. It's beautiful.

All of my Snipple Snapples

The first trickle is warm. I reach out for it. Her life is in there. In the dark, under the moonlight where the light goes from moon to curtain to dark room to black with the whole night out there being quiet so we can enjoy the breeze I take her life here where only our skin is shining, one small drop.

"Hmm, I'm bleeding."
"I know, I like it."
"You would, silly vampire. Only I get to drink my blood."

Then she takes her own life ...and sucks on it. She smiles and everything is in that. The temperature of the room raises a few degrees, the black starts to dark blue. I get up with her in my lap holding tight like a little monkey and close the curtains. We walk to the refrigerator like this. She's looking in my ears.

"Dave?"
"Yes, sweetheart."
"It's just that I'm looking in your head...."

I grab the ice cubes.

"Uhhummm?"

She gives me three little kisses on the cheek to my eyelid.

"....And there's nothing in there."

I make us each a glass of cold ice tea (this is making me thirsty). She's in a particular place, like a magnet it begins to pull. Soon I'm touching her.

"That's because I spend all my time thinking about you. All the other thoughts got jealous and left but now you're here. Of course there's nothing in my head. Here take your ice tea."

"And are you thinking of me now?"

We both take long hard drinks gulping it down, letting the cool fill us up.

"Uhh-hmmm."

I set the glasses down and grab hold of her rump with both hands. She kisses my forehead.

"I felt you were."

She jumps off onto the blue floor, grabs me by my hand where I'm fixed on the spot and pulls us towards the bedroom.

"Come on lets enjoy what's left of the night before the sun comes up and ruins everything."

Damn, that girl's lovely.

"I hate the sun." I say with a smile.
"Me too."

For some reason, just the hell of it I suppose, I start jumping on the bed. She bites down then flickers towards a smile, shakes her hair out and kicks back to a leap forward. The door slams with a bang. Here we're jumping. She's smiling. I feel silly and I love her. Someday she'll probly kill me. The moon's still there. It's quiet, everyone's dead asleep and it's great here behind closed doors.

15. The Struggle

You work hard. You dream hard. You wonder when it's gunna come. But some people never make it. You can work hard all your life. Some folks are just unlucky. Sometimes you care too much. Good people aren't necessarily on the front page. Good people might spend their lives slaving away and every second of everything they got trying to make a change just to rot away, just to have lived and never ascend. This isn't kindergarten. There's no systematic, Sunday school scales to weigh the righteous thoughts of do-gooders on. There's no one on earth that knows you're right. You need a knife. You need running shoes and a chess wreck mind. Good fuck, this earth is evil and God is going to wipe it clean away. You think us nice simple minded folk who just want to make the world a better place are ever going to succeed when God, our God, the one we worship and serve and strive to be like and please, you think you can accomplish anything when he's working against you with a breath you call the weight of life, the struggle you feel to move forward? Get a knife and cut short the breath of God. Run till the end. Do everything you can to make this crippled world something to walk on. Die and let it fall away. Then, when you stand in front of God waiting to be judged tell him you think that he's wrong. That you come from the soil. That you're family's worked hard all their lives and you may not be perfectionists but you got kids. They need a future. You need money. You got ideas. You don't have the time for theory. I want utopia now!

He'll laugh. Laugh so hard at you, scruff you're hair. You make me smile. That world is for the pushharders, the corner bomb builder blow this shit up I need a tunnel cutters. That world is for the wills. Whoever will take it will take it. If you can't take what it takes to take everything you want then you won't ever have anything worth stealing. Oh, you make me laugh. God'll hurt your feelings. No one's gunna tell him that he shouldn't and anyone that does just won't get a breath.

16. Dermes en Autumn

If it wasn't humid, the water'd get you when the snow melts. Bout the only time it's dry is autumn. One month there's hardly any rain. Autumn is wet too, but the air is crisp, breathable, livable. Winter's crisp but it's too damn cold. Likely to freeze. The spring just blends into the summer, and summer... I gave up on summer. It's a fucking rain forest. So I might move to California. I got some kids down there. I got some grandkids. I reckon before too long I'll have some great ones.

I got a full head of hair. Just lucky. Some folks lose their hair before thirty. I ain't yet turned 75. A lot of people think that's old. For the people who give up, 75 is well past dying age. But I'm alive and I never felt like that person in the mirror was me if I wasn't bleeding.

Leon McConnell

I stay young. I stay alive. I work. They had to force me to retire. Now I sit around and drink coffee, spend a lot of time on the internet. But I find that I can't stay in this place for too long. It's too quiet. It's been just me out here since my wife left me. That was twenty odd years ago.

Suppose I should move to the city. Well that's what they call it. It's really just a gas station surrounded by houses, maybe 20, maybe 30 or so. Maybe they got a couple video stores too. It's right on past the creek. That's thirty minutes from here. The creek rises with all this rain, and a man's late fees can really start to add up. I can't get to town sometimes but I don't like going there anyway. It reminds me of all the people I don't like. It's a silly town. These people believe in codswallop. Small folk got their head in their ass.

I live next door to my brother, but we don't talk much. He's about a five minute walk away. I fell once in my truck moving some furniture. Damn near broke my back. Lucky he came by.

I'm getting to that I don't know what to do. I was working and flirting and lifting the girls' skirts up. Now I'm an old man. I'm gonna have to trade it in; this quiet house, my deer, my grapes, my underground spring, these acres, my car, my cars. I'm gonna have to trade it in for a bed at my daughter's house. Then when she gets tired of me, I'll go stay at my son's. Then when he gets tired of me, I'll go back like before. Maybe my grandkids will have a home soon. They're growing up. It's just too quiet. This place is too wet. A man needs to die in the sun amidst the voices of the people who love him.

I've been through wars. I was a fighter pilot. Got married. I was an awful dad. Thank goodness the bitch I married was an even worse mom or my kids would've never stopped by. It takes a person time to get perspective. I was a bit too hard but that was just my way. I had been in the military. I am the great great grandson of Grover Cleveland, President of America, the United ones of...those states.

Well, I fucked up. So I tried again. I got some stepkids, and they liked me a little more than my own kids did. I wasn't so strict cuz I

All of my Snipple Snapples

didn't care so much cuz they weren't mine. So they had a bit more freedom. That was probly what they needed. My kids liked these kids, and my wife liked my kids. So things were okay.

I was a scientist. I still get calls from N.A.S.A. asking me how the damn signals fire in that telescope cuz they're not seeing shit. Outer space is dark, I tell 'em, or maybe the problem's this... That usually sorts them out.

Pussy was my past time. Had that stroke two years ago, kind of scared the girl. She pushed me off and called 911. I had to find a new hole to dig. The more I fucked, the deeper I dug my grave. It currently rests at 5' 2". I got a few more piles of dirt left in me.

The doctor said he'd never saw that. I am part of medical history. After two weeks I fully recovered. That has never happened. Most strokes go blind or dumb. I am a full human being ...and that's God. It's just God showing people things go well. I'm happy to be used for something. I always did trust God. You know, things go well, things go bad ...that's life. That's okay. There's nothing better.

When I was a boy I had five brothers and we was in the great depression. It's hard to feed your kids, let alone finding food when you're so depressed. One day a big ol' box of tapioca fell off the railroad train and me & my brothers carried it home. It was big. We ate tapioca for a year. It's a hell of a lot better than starving. I still eat tapioca. It tastes good. Was I making a point ? Oh yeah, If you can't see it you're fucking dumb. Oh yeah. I'm happy to be alive. I'm happy to be alive.

17. Fisher, Illinois circa 1983

Ma says the birds don't come around any more
Because someone put poison in their food
I look out the window
And I don't see any birds
Maybe they're dead
I remember this time last year
I used to see all the birdies
I would wake up in the afternoon

Leon McConnell

Around ten or so
And we would go for a walk through the field
Mama don't let me walk through that field no more
She says, "These are dark days."
Said, "God don't mean for no one to be like that."
She don't know, but I go through there sometimes
And I look at where it used to be
I just stand there with my hands in my pockets
Staring till the sun goes down
Then I walk home
It makes me cold inside to think like that
These long orange August sunsets drive some folk crazy
He still comes around sometimes
I see him
Folks say he's hiding
I figure people like that
They can't be around regular people
We just don't get along with each other
He knocks on my window sometimes when I'm sleepin
But I don't say nuthin though
He'll know me if he looks at me
I think he knows I seen him
I was walking on the field when he finished
I can't sleep at night seeing things like that
He ran, naked
He was covered in blood
She was lying there
Pieces of her missing
And marks like a dog had bit her
I sat there for a while
I reached out to touch it
See if it was real
My finger fell into her
Lying there
I closed my eyes
They took her away eventually
I looked up outside of her
And saw him looking at me.
He was hiding behind a tree

Just got up and walked home
It's creepy like that around here now

18. At Work Today

When I was a kid all I knew was one story buildings and liquor stores. LA stretched out so far, everything was flat little houses. Then I got this job running wire on construction sites. The pay wasn't much more than taco bell but every day I was in Brentwood, Malibu, Beverly Hills. Here was this whole other side to life I'd never seen. Their city was beautiful. I remember the first time I saw a deer crossing the street in Los Angeles. It was PCH by the lagoon and this buck comes jumping out of the bushes. Bob hit the brakes and this fucking deer is all over traffic. This big ol' catering truck don't see it. Smash!!!! The fucking deer goes bouncing off their fender and across the highway like a ping pong ball behind the car in front of us. We ran over him. Both of us heard the bones crunch and his body knock against the under carriage. I turned around to look at the dead deer in the rearview mirror when miracles of miracles. It got up and was alive. Yay! And jumped home a little sore. Bob said nah. They do that, go off into the woods to die. Something about dignity. I loved that job. The houses were amazing.

19. Cancer Talk

I've gone out to the riverbed to grab a seat and watch the city sleep, to dangle from dirty railroad tracks above wasted dying shopping carts. The water worms its way through wheels & eyes. I pick up a railroad spike and toss it in to hear the splash but pretend it's a bouquet.

The water doesn't rush hard enough to listen to. I only hear the sunshine. The candy warm pink rays flicker like snake tongues on my skin and I hear it all with my ears. It says "I'll turn my back & you can take this city while it sleeps. you can pull me out the sky, take a bite and be a star yourself. Crunch on the apple, kick up the river. Live live live."

That's cancer talk. My skin don't shine. My eyes don't burn. I feel at home in the dark. I wouldn't mind a corona. I'm not one likely to blow up. I'd rather be this river here, not too loud but always flowin. I won't change directions but I'll change my course and if I want this city I'll take it, regardless of the concrete beds they've laid me in.

I burn sun. I burn. I burn like books and blues songs, torch ballads & toasty marshmallows. I blow up like elation. I sunshine like happiness and glow like kind smiles. You're trying to sell me something I've already got. You're alone in outer space while I'm fire down here, telling stories to the river and tucking the city in to sleep.

20. Self Portrait

I'd like to write something down and not romanticize it, not really stylize it in anyway. I'm not out to manipulate you or even entertain you. I just want to tell you what happened to me when I was young, with little to no experience, coming from a bad place with no idea of where to go, just knowing I needed to get out.

I fell in love over the internet, over the phone, with a girl in Sydney, Australia. I lived in Los Angeles, on the actual literal border of Lakewood and Cerritos ...almost all the way to Orange County. This all happened in 1999, the year my family got the internet and the world opened up to me.

I'd always been a reader. Obviously, the fact that I'm writing this conveys some notion that I have a predilection for letters. So I took to typing with strangers online like a natural.

I began talking to this girl over there when I was 21, almost 22. I'd never kissed anyone. I wasn't shy. I was in theater. I was a performer. I was on the college radio station and rapped in front of everyone at backyard parties. I'd just never kissed anyone, let alone gone any further. I'd never had any sort of girl anything. Not for a lack of interest on my part or from girls in general. I was just never going to jump off the edge without being pushed.

My sister sometimes surmises that maybe I have some sort of Asperger's. I don't. I just had weird social issues that I had to work very hard at to get through. So when I met someone my age that I could talk to ...on a keyboard, way far away on the other side of the planet, something clicked and I made my way over yonder.

She picked me up in a cute little poodle skirt and I lost my virginity about an hour after I had my first kiss in the back of a taxi heading to Paddington in the middle of the night.

When she'd go to work, I'd sit in her room and read. I remember the rain pouring like I'd never seen it pour in LA. In a room facing some alley called Victoria Street, I realized that maybe I'd made a mistake. If I had been a normal person I would have started fucking sometime in adolescence, but we all have these quirks that make us human.

I like my version of me. Ignoring sex took me so many places I would have never had made it to if I were lost in some girl's room. And then there I was, lost in some girl's room; dim light bulbs, grey skies, dusty corners, damp walls, a definite lack of order.

I had to get out of LA and being with Sari in Sydney taught me so much. This failure, this supreme failure, is the ground that I was born in, the ash you need for growing a fiery bird. I became an adult because I had to care for myself. I became permanently single because I gave being a husband my all.

Now there's an old friend who lives across town and I know her in ways no one else can, in ways I know no one else. I know her through us crawling out of childhood together, through trying our hardest to build a world together, through crumbling, through apocalypse, through sorted rubble and finding friends, through running like cats after mice and getting drunk, too drunk. I know her through worry, through years and years of it. I know her from across the way, the way city blocks drift and time sort of melts when you recollect it.

I didn't know any of that would be coming when I was sitting in her bedroom, watching the rain, wishing it was warmer. It's weird how the rain can hide so much and when you let it, whole pages of your life just wash away.

21. The Borracho of Christmas Past

I found a bike abandoned on Hollywood Boulevard Christmas Eve while standing at the bus stop. The breaks didn't work but I rode it a few miles in the rain for fun before dragging it down to the train and back to my apartment over the bridge.

Today I took it to the bike shop on Cesar Chávez by Shakey's. The dude in there was busy fixing another bike so I just waited outside for my turn. The neighborhood was definitely changing. Old Mexico East LA had become frosted. It wasn't just gentrification. The people changed. Times change. I felt comfortable in this juxtaposition. The sidewalk was a grey zone.

This borracho came out the bike shop and jumped when he saw me. I said hello. You never know how people are going to react. I try to keep trouble away but am always ready for guests. He was frazzled. I'm big, very big, 6'3" 250, hair down my back, leaning against a wall, waiting for homedude to fix my bike. His synapses had trouble firing in the alcohol but at some point he seemed to realize I'm a friendly behemoth.

I asked him how his Christmas went. This particular borracho is of the storytelling sort, just like one of the men who raised me. Easily, he let it all unfold. Christmas started at King Taco on Soto and Cesar Chávez. He grabbed his pozole and King Cobras and was catching the party bus to Morongo. It stops right across the street. I'd see old people boarding it every morning as I pedaled to work.

Whilst enjoying the festive Aire Conditioning of Yule, our man's wave hit the brakes and the bus driver demanded to see his $25 ticket. Here is one of those points where the borracho probly changed his story so we think he's the most lovable and likable person on the planet because for no reason at all the bus driver called the police on him somewhere out in Riverside and he was dragged off the bus.

My familiarity with arrest procedure for alcoholic homeless types goes back a long way, kindergarten at least. At no point was I worried for my new friend. I mean here he was standing right next to Shakey's with me on a fine December's end. He did eight hours in the drunk tank but was worried about how this would affect his probation. Thank God for Christmas, the officers didn't even bother booking him, just locked him up then let him go.

It was at this point that the fellow told me his name and I told him mine and we bonded over both being Cancer/Leo cusps born just a few days apart on opposite ends of the divide. This is a true story, retold word for word how it happened, unembellished but not spit shined at least a little. The truth ballasts all my flights of verbal fancy lest the story float away. I'm not gunna tell you his name.

He reminded me of my uncle Mark. I'm sure Uncle Mark told stories like this on sidewalks in South Gate to teenagers and other alcoholics where we grew up. I'm sure he'd also been kicked out of a jail in Riverside on Christmas and stumbled into an "IHOP's" then begged some white woman to buy him one pancake, just one. The key to successful begging is never to get too greedy. Never tell people what you want, just ask for less than what you think they're willing to give you.

The Uncle Mark in front of me, who I was happy to spend this holiday moment with, Uncle Mark checked out years ago, not every borracho makes the stretch, miraculously woke up somehow in East LA the next day with $100 in his pocket. He doesn't know how. God is looking out for him. God loves drunks and old cats. They defy logic.

The police rolled past in an SUV and our guy got nervous. I figured they were just turning the corner onto Hollenbeck and didn't want to bother stopping anyone so close to home. He took the slightest security in the fact that I had long hair so the cops were less likely to stop him then he rambled on about drunk stuff that made no fucking sense. I couldn't make out all the words. Before long he wanted to make sure I was from LA. He couldn't trust someone who'd just crawled out of the cold with all this information. As I caught a whiff of the brain fry I'm happy to have never seen in my own particular borracho, my interest in the conversation waned.

The ghost of Uncle Mark stopped talking to me. All that was left was this guy and I felt sorry for him. I didn't wonder what made him this way because it doesn't matter. This is the way he is. Accept that or don't. I didn't want to be there anymore. The sidewalk stopped being a place I loved like it was five minutes ago when the borracho had begun spinning his tale. I wished him a happy new year and rode off. Probly bump into him again someday soon but he probly won't remember me.

www.ingramcontent.com/pod-product-compliance
Lightning Source LLC
Chambersburg PA
CBHW032143040426
42449CB00005B/378